What current students think about
*The Complete University Guide: Stud...*

'The book provides excellent advice and guidance to potential students who may initially be put off applying to university because of the costs involved. It also provides great reassurance to current students such as myself who are worried about their existing financial situation.'

'The book covers an excellent diversity of issues from student loans to international students and those considering a gap year. In particular, I thought that the "Words you need to know" section of the book was very useful. When I first began to apply to university, I found the whole process a bit daunting as there were a lot of confusing words flying about, so this glossary of terms is very valuable for a first time student.'

'The Bursary table is very helpful to potential undergraduates as many do choose their university depending on the financial sources available, so the table provides a great, easy way to compare each university.'

'The book will be of great use to both students and parents worried about finance. The layout is good and I appreciated the student facts, other students' comments and the snippets of information about famous people who studied at various universities.'

'I think the section on "Crossing Borders" will be of particular use. I considered studying in Wales and would have had no knowledge on where to start with applying for student finance. Also, the list of charities which may help out students with bursaries/scholarships was completely new to me.'

**Bernard Kingston** has degrees in chemistry from the Universities of Leicester and Sussex. He is the Principal Partner in Mayfield University Consultants and was Director of Careers and later of International Affairs at the University of Sheffield. He is a past President of the Association of Graduate Careers Advisory Services.

**Nicola Chalton** graduated from the University of Reading and University College London. She has worked as an editor and publisher, and has written and contributed to several books, including *How to Improve Your Memory in 8 Simple Steps*.

IN ASSOCIATION WITH

# UCAS

The **COMPLETE UNIVERSITY** Guide

# STUDENT FINANCE

## Your guide to loans, bursaries, grants, tuition fees and preparing your own budget

**RIGHT WAY**

Supported by

*PRICEWATERHOUSECOOPERS*

Constable & Robinson Ltd
3 The Lanchesters
162 Fulham Palace Road
London W6 9ER
www.constablerobinson.com

First published by Right Way, an imprint of Constable & Robinson, 2009

A copy of the British Library Cataloguing in Publication Data is available from the British Library

ISBN: 978-0-7160-2229-9

Printed and bound in the EU

1  3  5  7  9  10  8  6  4  2

**Publisher's note**
Every possible effort has been made to ensure that the information contained in this book is accurate at the time of going to press, and the publishers and authors cannot accept responsibility for any errors or omissions, however caused. No responsibility for loss or damage occasioned to any person acting, or refraining from action, as a result of the material in this publication can be accepted by the editors, the publisher or any of the authors.

## Acknowledgements and thanks

We wish to offer our best personal thanks to Professor Robert Burgess, Vice-Chancellor of the University of Leicester for his Foreword to the guide, to David Jobbins, Head of Education at Candlestar Ltd, for setting the scene in the Introduction, and to those undergraduates at the Universities of Aston, Leicester and Sussex who have willingly shared their insights and tips.

We would also like to thank all those who have helped in the publication of this book, especially UCAS and PricewaterhouseCoopers for their support; our colleagues, Cicely Frew and Alison Patterson at The Complete University Guide; Paul Higgs, Patrick Smith, Conn O'Prey, Rhydian Harry, Bryan Hunter and Miriam Craven in the four UK Administrations for their technical advice; and Claire McGhee at the Student Loans Company.

The publishers wish to thank the following for giving their permission to publish material: Universities UK for a selection of facts from their booklet *90 out of 90, A window into the UK's universities*; The NatWest Bank for the results of their Student Living Index 2008; Justin Burns of My Property Guide for information on student accommodation; James Ball at the *The Grocer* magazine for food price data; and Simon Thompson at accommodationforstudents.com for student rental figures.

# Contents

# Foreword

Preparing to go to university is a really exciting time as students choose their preferred course and select an institution. Alongside this 'new' experience come a variety of issues that need to be resolved including whether to take a gap year, how to get a part-time job and how to manage your finances. Yet headlines in the popular press suggest that finance could be very problematic as students need to understand loans, grants, bursaries and fees in an attempt to avoid student debt. On this basis, clear guidance is needed for students and their parents.

Bernard Kingston and Nicola Chalton have produced an excellent guide to student finance as they address many of the major issues on which students want advice. This book is clear, concise and easy to follow and is a good addition to The Complete University Guide stable. It deserves to become the definitive guide for students.

The authors very helpfully segment the information into income and expenditure and cover a wide range of issues. The section on income includes different types of arrangements relating to full-time, part-time and distance learning students as well as dealing with support for students with dependants and disabled students. There are also sections that highlight the availability of awards, bursaries and scholarships, and an all important section on hardship funds to which many students are entitled but are sadly ill informed. This book also discusses career development loans and employer sponsorship before moving on to suggest ways to manage expenditure. There are sections on budgeting for living costs, dealing with banks, managing your money and most importantly survival tips for students. Throughout the text there are facts and figures, handy hints and advice on other sources of help.

All together this book provides excellent advice from the authors with helpful tips from finance to food, gap year to sponsorship, accommodation to travel and much more. The authors also take great care to portray the realities of student life using quotations from current students who suggest practical ways to handle financial problems. Finally, the guide contains a valuable series of appendices that usefully summarise details on the bursaries and scholarships that are available in all UK universities. To have all this material collected together in one place with links to a website containing further information make this book essential reading and a must for school and college libraries.

May 2009

Professor Robert Burgess
Vice-Chancellor
University of Leicester

# Introduction

Your years at university are an opportunity to study, make new friends and develop as an individual. For most people it is a once-in-a-lifetime experience that will influence the rest of your life.

Finances should be a part – but only a part – of that process. A necessary part because learning through experience how to handle money and keep your finances on an even keel will equip you for the bigger challenges that will arise in later years. But a part that should not dominate the rest.

If there was a golden age it was when the state paid tuition fees for the relatively small proportion of (mainly) middle class young people who attended university and qualified for a means-tested Maintenance Grant that enabled them largely to ignore money matters and to get on with their university years in the expectation of emerging debt-free into a world where they had the pick of the jobs.

The reforms of the 1980s effectively phased out the grant by freezing its value and introduced the concept of regulated loans to cover living costs. But tuition remained free at the point of delivery – the taxpayer picked up the bill.

Students gained lifetime benefits from their education and society gained from an increase – a dramatic increase – in the number of young people with a university education. But the universities felt economically squeezed – and diplomatically but successfully campaigned for a direct return for the volume of students they taught.

Shortly after gaining power in 1997, New Labour introduced fees that were payable upfront on registration (limited to £1,250 a year and subject to a parental means test). In 2006, despite opposition from within its own ranks, the government allowed universities in England to charge variable fees subject to a maximum of £3,000 (now £3,225). The essential difference – apart from the higher maximum – was that the fees, rather than being payable during a student's course, could be added to their student loan and are repayable after graduation (subject to an income threshold of £15,000 a year).

The government and its supporters argued that this removed the means test from the fee and encouraged wider access by sections of society that were under-represented in higher education. The means test lives on in the distribution of grants aimed at students from lower- and middle-income backgrounds.

But the vast majority of English universities set fees at the maximum, in line with their argument that the universities were underfunded. The 'market' predicted for higher education is to be found in the complex of scholarships and bursaries that universities are required to make available under access arrangements that are an integral part of the plan.

The review of the impact of the policy is unlikely to be completed before the next general election. The Conservatives have said they recognise the value of tuition fees as a funding mechanism but want to see evidence that the returns are enhancing the student experience.

So far, however, there is little or no evidence that despite the warnings, the introduction of variable fees has had any impact on the thirst for a university education. 'Uni' is now a rite of passage for thousands of young people irrespective of social class and income, but whether the ambitious targets set when the new arrangements were introduced have succeeded in encouraging wider participation by under-represented groups is still open to question.

Some observers suggest that the UK – and specifically England – is moving steadily closer to the United States model where tuition fees have been the norm. But there is a long way to go before top UK universities emulate the private 'Ivy League' universities' astronomic tuition fees mitigated by subsidies from their endowment incomes to academically-gifted but financially challenged students.

Anyone wondering how variable fees might work need only look to Australia. In the late 1980s, its pioneering Higher Education Contribution Scheme introduced a flat rate tuition fee covering part of the cost of a degree course, with the option of repayment through the tax system on graduation. In 1996 the initial flat rate was replaced by a three-tier variable fee, with the levels determined by broad expectations of income on graduation. Fees were deregulated in 2005.

This near-free market is probably too recent to draw conclusions on the impact on student participation, particularly as the new Labor government is introducing its own changes.

But both the US and Australia are in dramatic contrast with continental Europe where tuition fees are virtually unheard-of, and students are able to draw on a variety of social benefits to meet their costs.

However, universally, there is a shift towards replacement of personal intellectual development with greater relevance to the labour market in students' motivation. A generation ago, a defined cluster of occupations were deemed to be professions, legally requiring a degree. Now, however, many more jobs require a degree by custom if not by law.

This shift has many benefits, enhancing many careers by opening them up to the critical values associated with university education.

As the cost of a university degree to the graduate has escalated, interest has centred on the costs and benefits of attending university. A university student potentially forgoes three years of earning in the jobs market, and additionally acquires debts that have to be repaid. When the government introduced 'top-up' fees, it drew attention to research suggesting that over their working life, graduates would earn around £400,000 more than non-graduates.

But Universities UK, the universities' representative body, later disputed this figure for the 'graduate premium', proposing a lifetime advantage of just £160,000 compared to those with A-levels.

There are other benefits too – the Organisation for Economic Co-operation and Development has found that university graduates tend to live healthier, more fulfilling and stable lives than their degree-less counterparts.

It is no secret that many of the UK's prestigious universities would like to see the ceiling rise beyond £10,000 – with some wanting the ceiling to be removed completely. But a 2009 report for Universities UK predicted that students would be deterred once fees reached £7,000 and instead proposed £6,500 or less.

Students entering university in 2010 should escape any rises. But even so the day of the debt-free student is probably long gone. Forecasting debt levels with accuracy is virtually impossible, but could be in excess of £15,000.

With these figures in mind, you will need clear and accurate advice to help you make your choice of course, university and career, and offer practical guidance to navigate the everyday decisions necessary to keep your finances on an even keel, keep debts manageable and build a solid foundation for the future. This guide has been written specifically to help you to address these crucial matters, clearly and confidently. With it you should be able to focus on the real challenges of university life.

# How to use this book

Use this book to work out the costs of going to university, to find out how to apply for student funding, and to learn how to manage your own student budget. It is particularly relevant for students from the UK or overseas who are beginning first degree courses in England, Northern Ireland, Scotland or Wales – and their parents or carers.

Although the book focuses primarily on university students and does not cover funding for those students attending further education (FE) and some higher education (HE) colleges, such students will find that the advice given here on part-time and vacation work, taking a gap year, finding rented accommodation, opening a bank account, and managing a budget will be of help to them. Information for FE and HE students on funding that may be available to them, such as the Adult Learning Grant (ALG) and Discretionary Support Funds, can be found on the Directgov website.

The first part of the book sums up the student funding system in the UK and investigates why many students are building up debts. Part 2 – **Income** – covers all the various loans, grants and bursaries available for undergraduates from the public purse, and explains how you can supplement your income through part-time and holiday employment, other awards and sponsorship.

Part 3 – **Expenditure** – covers tuition fees and living costs (maintenance) while you are a student, and gives tips on how to save money. Income and Expenditure are the key areas you'll need to consider when planning your student budget – you'll find advice on how to budget in chapter 17. Throughout the book we've included comments from students giving their own views on student funding and tips for surviving at university.

## Changing arrangements

Financial arrangements for students are continually being updated. Most of the figures in this book are relevant to students beginning courses in 2009. Amounts for the following academic year are normally published in the period from the previous September through to March.

There is a commitment by the government to review all of the current student funding arrangements from 2010 onwards. Under the current arrangements, annual university tuition fees are susidised and capped, so they cannot rise above a certain level (£3,225 in 2009/10). However, the cap has already come under scrutiny. A BBC survey conducted among 53 university vice-chancellors found that cash-strapped universities are calling for a substantial increase in fees from the current annual maximum – necessary, they claim, if UK universities are to remain competitive in a global economy. Separate research by Universities UK also found that universities on average want fees to rise – to £6,500 a year. There are some who believe the cap should be removed altogether to create a market whereby institutions compete for students, in line with the system in the USA. The full fees at Harvard, for example, are over $30,000 a year. For the moment, no changes to the UK system have been agreed and the government is only committed to its review of the fee regime and to make sure that tuition fees at any level are not deterring individuals from coming to university.

For the latest news on this topic and other student funding matters, check with your student finance provider (websites on page 13) and the supporting website for this book (see below).

## Supporting website

www.thecompleteuniversityguide.co.uk This book has not come into being all on its own. It has evolved from a website covering all aspects of going to university: The Complete University Guide. This popular site has generated a whole range of student feedback, but a common theme around the complex topic of student finance has been the bewilderment of students faced by the array of options available to them and the different rules that apply to each. They also seemed to have little idea of how to plan a student budget. There was obviously a need for a clear and well thought out guide devoted to the subject.

The Complete University Guide offers the most comprehensive, independent, completely impartial, fully interactive and authoritative online guide to university education. It includes:

- an innovative, interactive University League Table which enables users to create bespoke rankings and select and compare universities
- university listings by 62 subjects
- advice on finance
- graduate salaries and prospects
- international student information and statistics
- advice on how to choose what to study, where to study and how to apply

- information and statistics on bursaries and scholarships
- profiles of universities and university cities
- information and unique ranking of sports facilities
- advice and statistics on safety, security and crime
- advice for parents

We recommend that you use the website alongside this book for:

- the latest news on loans, grants, scholarships, bursaries and other funding
- recommended links to help you find suitable accommodation, gap year projects, sponsorship, etc.
- a budget sheet which you can download when you come to plan your budget

The website will be updated with new information on student finance as it becomes available. Please check for updates.

## Words you need to know

There are several words that crop up regularly and have a particular meaning in the context of student finance. We've selected a few here to help you understand the information that follows. A full glossary can be found at the end of the book (page 236).

**Loan** Financial support which usually has to be re-paid.
**Grant** Financial support which is yours to keep.
**Tuition fee** The fee that your university charges for your tuition, sometimes known as 'top-up fee' or 'variable fee'.
**Tuition Fee Loan** A loan to cover the fees that your university charges. Sometimes known as the 'Student Loan for Tuition Fees' (or simply a 'Student Loan').
**Maintenance Loan** A loan towards your day-to-day living costs while at university (for example, accommodation, food, household bills, socialising and course materials). Sometimes known as

the 'Student Loan for Maintenance' (or simply a 'Student Loan').

**Maintenance Grant**  A grant towards the day-to-day living costs while at university. Sometimes known as a 'Student Grant' or a 'Special Support Grant'.

**Bursary/Scholarship**  A grant of financial aid awarded by a university or another organisation. It is normally based on need and/or exceptional ability. Universities often use the terms 'bursary' and 'scholarship' interchangeably.

**Hardship Funds**  Public funding administered by universities and distributed to students in financial need.

**Student finance provider**  The organisation responsible for dealing with applications from students for funding.

**Means-testing**  The process of investigating your household income to determine eligibility for financial assistance.

**Household income**  The income of your parents, or, if you are an independent student (page 72), your own income and that of your partner. How much you receive in Maintenance Loan, Maintenance Grant and other means-tested support will depend on your household income.

## UCAS – helping students into higher education

UCAS is responsible for managing applications to full-time undergraduate courses within UK higher education. Not only does it process more than two million applications every year, it also helps students to find their right course. To make things run as smoothly as possible, UCAS provides innovative online tools for students to manage applications and offers. See www.ucas.com for more information.

## PricewaterhouseCoopers LLP (PwC)

As one of the largest professional Services firms in the world, PricewaterhouseCoopers LLP (PwC) provides industry-focused assurance, tax, financial advisory, actuarial and consulting services to an enviable range of clients.

Proud to be voted the UK's number one employer in *The Times Top 100 Graduate Employers* survey for the last five years, PwC is the ideal employer for any budding business professional. www.pwc.com/uk/careers/

# PART 1: THE SYSTEM IN A NUTSHELL

First let's take a brief look at the system of student finance in the UK to give you a basic idea of the main types of funding available.

*Brian May, the lead guitarist of rock band Queen, studied Astrophysics at Imperial College London.*

 **1** **Support for students**

Undergraduates at most universities in the UK must pay a contribution towards their **tuition fees** (known as 'top-up fees' or 'variable fees') and pay in full for their living costs while they are studying – such as costs of accommodation, food, books, transport and entertainment. To help you finance your way through university the government has devised a system of **Student Loans** at a very low rate of interest (just covering inflation) to help towards the costs of living and any tuition fees. These loans don't have to paid back until after graduation, once you start earning £15,000 or more. Part of the loan to cover your living costs (known as a '**Maintenance Loan**') is means-tested or 'income assessed' – in other words, students from wealthier backgrounds get less.

There is also generous support for students from low-income families in the form of **grants** from the government and **bursaries** or **scholarships** from your university or college, extra help

**GRADUATION DEBT**
Recent surveys suggest that, on average, students might expect to graduate with a debt of £15,000 or more, most of it in Student Loans. But this hasn't stopped many students from graduating: in 2007/08 there were 334,890 first degree graduates, an increase of 5 per cent on the previous year.

for students with children or other dependants, and allowances for disabled students. These grants and bursaries don't need to be paid back, but they don't cover the whole cost of going to university, so even students from low-income families will need to take out a Maintenance Loan to cover their living expenses.

Many students work part-time during term time and full-time during the vacations to make ends meet and reduce their level of debt. Others keep their costs down by living at home, or by learning to live frugally, while accepting that they will perhaps have more debt to pay off during their working life.

### Student Talk

*'I am worried about being in debt at university, as it is quite a scary concept knowing that the money you are spending is only on loan... However, I don't think this should deter someone from going to university. In the long run I am at university to gain an education and a degree which will hopefully enable me to have a highly paid job in the future so that I can pay off my debts. At the end of this academic year I expect to have about £6,000 student debt, and when I leave I expect to have about £20,000 debt.'*

### Student Talk

'I am not really worried about getting into debt at university as it is inevitable. I don't expect to have an overdraft by the end of the academic year. I expect at least £25,000 worth of debt when I leave university.'

'I will get into debt but I'm not worried about it. The repayments are small, and will not affect me massively in the long run.'

'Prospective students should just be excited for the experience ahead of them, not dwelling on debt or whether you will be able to eat. Enough students make it work so there is nothing to say that you can't either.'

The Funding Councils for
England, Wales and Scotland
were established in 1992.
In the same year, polytechnics
gained university status.

## 2  Why you need to budget

You could be eligible for some or all of the following
support with your day-to-day living costs: a Maintenance Loan,
a Maintenance Grant, a non-repayable university bursary, and
also possibly help from your university Hardship Fund if you
get into financial difficulty. So, as well as help with tuition fees
if you have to pay them, your annual government and university support towards living costs could add up to £5,000–£7,000
(or £7,000–£9,000 if you are studying in London), depending
on your financial circumstances.

On the expenditure side, a student's cost of living over an academic year (including rent, food, course materials, socialising,
travel, laundry, phone, etc, but not including tuition fees) can typ-
ically mount up to around £10,000–12,000 (the higher figure in
London) and you still have to support yourself through the holidays. If you stay in rented accommodation during the vacations
you can add another £1,000–2,000 just in rent. Of course your
total living costs can soar if you aren't careful with your spending.

The upshot is that you are very likely to have a shortfall of
funds even after receiving all the government and university
funding you can get. The good news is that once you know
about the likely shortfall you can plan how to deal with it. For
example, you may decide to get a part-time job during term

time (chapter 13). Accommodation is the highest expense, especially in London. The Maintenance Loan is higher for London but the steep accommodation costs, particularly in the private sector where you generally pay rent during some vacations as well as term time, can use up your loan money very quickly. You are strongly advised to draw up a budget before beginning your course to help you keep costs under control.

### Student Talk

'I have kept my overdraft limit at £500 and I do not want to be using my full overdraft as it is difficult to get back on track. I will have about £12,000 debt by the end of the course, which sounds horrific to me.'

'I worry about debt quite a lot, although it's marginal in comparison to the experience I will receive and the qualification at the end of it all.'

# PART 2: INCOME

How much will you get from the public purse?
This part of the book is about mustering all the
resources you can lay your hands on to finance your
way through university. Here you'll find details of the
various loans, grants and bursaries available from the
government, and other sources of income – the vast
majority of students have to rely on savings, earnings
from part-time/vacation work, overdrafts and the
generosity of family and friends to get by. There is also
information on sponsorship by employers, gap year
activities and working while you study.

# 3   Some preliminaries

## Crossing borders

Which UK country you come from and which one you plan to study in can have a marked effect on your pocket. This is because there are important differences between the student finance systems in England, Northern Ireland, Scotland and Wales. For example, Scottish students who choose to study in Scotland have their tuition fees paid for them, whereas if they choose to study in England they must pay fees to the English university, but will qualify for a Tuition Fee Loan to cover them.

Although universities always welcome students from different UK countries, there have been concerns about increased migration across borders of undergraduates seeking refuge from higher fees or less generous grants and bursaries. The Scots, already facing a shortfall in recruitment of home-grown medical staff, have a particular concern about the potential for increased numbers coming into their medical schools from south of the border. As a consequence, they try to help Scottish students staying in their own country by paying their tuition fees, while incomers generally have to pay the fees themselves.

It's important to weigh up the actual cost of 'crossing borders' as it's not just about the level of fees you pay. For example, many Scottish degrees could involve an extra year of study and

during that year you will incur expenses that you might not
have incurred on a similar course at an English university. The
cost of flights or train journeys to and from your home three or
more times a year may also be a consideration!

The table below shows the movement of students who 'cross
borders' to study in a UK country other than their own. The
most significant movement of students is from Wales to study
in England while the most dispersed are students from
Northern Ireland.

**WHERE STUDENTS CHOOSE TO STUDY IN THE UK (PERCENTAGES OF ACCEPTED APPLICANTS)**

| Home country | University country | | | |
| --- | --- | --- | --- | --- |
| | England | Wales | Scotland | Northern Ireland |
| England | 96% | 3% | 1% | Less than 1% |
| Wales | 30% | 70% | Less than 1% | Less than 1% |
| Scotland | 6% | Less than 1% | 94% | Less than 1% |
| Northern Ireland | 24% | Less than 1% | 8% | 67% |
| Other EU | 76% | 4% | 18% | 2% |
| Non-EU | 84% | 4% | 12% | Less than 1% |

(Source: UCAS 2008 – the figures have been rounded up for simplicity)

Detailed financial arrangements for those of you planning to
cross a UK border to study are included in the chapters that follow, along with the more usual option of staying in your home
country. Chapters 3 to 7 set out the general principles of stu-

dent finance and should be read by all prospective students. These chapters use the example of students who normally live in England and are planning to begin a full-time undergraduate course anywhere in the UK in 2009. If you do not live in England, chapter 8 will then give you the key differences in the Welsh, Northern Irish and Scottish systems, and the special rules that apply for non-UK EU and international students. You should also bookmark and use the relevant weblinks below.

**STUDENT FINANCE PROVIDERS**
If you normally live in England, Northern Ireland, Scotland or Wales, and are studying anywhere in the UK, your application for student finance will be dealt with by the student finance provider in the country where you normally live:
- Student Finance England: www.direct.gov.uk/studentfinance
- Student Finance Northern Ireland: www.studentfinanceni.co.uk
- Student Finance Wales: www.studentfinancewales.co.uk
- Student Awards Agency for Scotland (SAAS): www.saas.gov.uk
For non-UK EU students:
- Student Finance Services European Team, via: www.direct.gov.uk/studentfinance-EU

## Special cases
The funding arrangements for specialised courses and students who don't fit the standard profile are covered in chapter 9. This is where you will find information on student finance for:

- independent students (page 72)
- students with dependants (page 74)
- disabled students (page 75)
- part-time and distance learning students (page 76)
- sandwich courses incorporating a work placement (page 80)
- language courses and studying abroad (page 83)

- Foundation year courses (page 88)
- courses in Dentistry and Medicine, the Allied Health Professions, Nursing and Midwifery (pages 89–94)
- Social Work courses (page 94)
- Initial Teacher Training (ITT) courses (page 96)

## Parental financial role

The head of one university tells the story of a photographer at graduation asking the student to place a hand on her parent's shoulder, only to hear the parent's riposte, 'Wouldn't it be more appropriate to have a hand in my pocket!' It is an apocryphal tale but one which will ring true for many parents, given the financial support required these days. Student funding from the government and universities is part means-tested. In other words, families who can afford it are expected to contribute financially to their child's university education. Parents of Scottish-domiciled students are assessed to contribute more than other parents in the UK, but on the other hand their sons and daughters have no tuition fees to pay if they choose to study in Scotland.

**MUST PARENTS CONTRIBUTE?**

Parents assessed under the student funding arrangements in the UK are not legally required to contribute to their child's university education. However, the student finance provider will assume that parents are making contributions if they are assessed to do so. If parents don't contribute, then their offspring are unlikely to have enough money to cover their living costs while at university.

# 4 Student Loans

Government funding for UK students consists primarily of Student Loans administered by the Student Loans Company Ltd (SLC). You will be eligible for two Student Loans from the government: a **Tuition Fee Loan** to cover any tuition fees you have to pay and a **Maintenance Loan** to help with your day-to-day living costs (accommodation, food, clothes, travel, etc). Student Loans don't have to be paid back until you've left your course and started earning over £15,000 a year – allowing you to study first and pay back when you're working. You pay a low rate of interest on the loan which covers only the cost of inflation: in real terms what you repay is no more than what you borrow. Compare this to a commercial bank or building society loan and you'll see that the interest rate on a Student Loan is much lower. The government makes no profit at all on a Student Loan and in fact subsidises (pays towards) the total cost of your studies.

### STUDENT NUMBERS ARE RISING

When Student Loans were first introduced many people thought that student numbers would plummet. In fact the number of applications to courses at higher education institutions in the UK has tended to increase each year since then. In 2008, 456,627 full-time students were accepted onto undergraduate courses, a record 10.4 per cent increase on the previous year. (Source: UCAS, 2008)

## ● Do you qualify?

To qualify for a Student Loan you will need to satisfy certain criteria, such as your residency (you must normally live in the UK), your course must be of the right type (for example, a first degree course such as a BSc, BA, BEd) and the university or college must be either publicly funded or privately funded but running individual courses that receive public funding. See further details in the booklet *Higher Education Student Finance – How you are assessed and paid*, available at www.direct. gov.uk/studentfinance.

> **LOAN TIP**
>
> You don't have to take out Student Loans – but the vast majority of students do. We recommend that you give the matter serious consideration as commercial loans or borrowing through a credit card are much more expensive ways to raise funds. Student Loans are likely to form a significant part of your income, are essentially interest free and you can always put the loan money in an interest-bearing account.

## ● Tuition Fee Loan

This loan is not means-tested. In other words, how much you get is not based on your household income – everyone gets the same. It is available to all UK undergraduate students on full-time courses who have to pay tuition fees (page 127) and also to other EU undergraduate students. The loan is

**PRIVATE UNIVERSITY**

The University of Buckingham is the only private university in the UK. Founded in 1976 and run independently of direct government support, it is based on the American model of private 'ivy-league' institutions.

intended to cover the full cost of the tuition fee charged by your university. So if your university levies an annual tuition fee of £3,225 for your particular course (i.e. the maximum fee allowed in 2009/10), then you can have a Tuition Fee Loan for £3,225 to cover it in full. The loan is paid by your student finance provider direct to the university where you are studying. If you apply for a Tuition Fee Loan, check with your university to confirm what fee you will be charged so you can ask for the appropriate amount in your loan application.

Scottish students (and EU students who are not from the UK) studying in Scotland have their tuition fees paid for them and so the Tuition Fee Loan does not apply. Part-time and distance learning students are not eligible for Tuition Fee Loans (page 76) except some part-time teacher training students (page 97).

**CHANGING COURSE**
If you leave your course or transfer to a new one, this may affect the financial support you can get if you take another course in the future. Talk to your university and student finance provider as soon as possible if you want to change course. If the fees are higher than on your current course, you may be able to apply for an additional Tuition Fee Loan.

## Maintenance Loan

The Maintenance Loan is to help cover your living costs during the academic year. It is part means-tested and available to all full-time UK undergraduate students in all four countries of the UK. The various factors taken into consideration in calculating your loan include your household income, whether or not you plan to live at home and where you intend

CASH TIP

**Bear in mind that any Maintenance Loan payments due could take a week or more to reach your bank account so make sure you have some cash to tide you over the first few days at university.**

to study. For example, the loan is lowest if you live outside London and decide to stay at home, and highest if you go to a university in London and stay in rented accommodation. The loan will usually be paid straight into your bank or building society account in three instalments (monthly in Scotland), the first at the start of the academic year.

## How much do you get?

The good news is that roughly 72 per cent of the Maintenance Loan for students starting in 2009/10 comes to you regardless of your family circumstances. The remaining 28 per cent or so depends on your household income. Students from higher-income families won't receive the full loan, and your parents are expected to make up the difference, though this is not compulsory. For lower-income families, part of the loan may be replaced by a **Maintenance Grant** which does not need to be repaid (page 26). The table opposite shows the maximum amount you can get in the first year of a standard undergraduate course (i.e. an academic year of around 30 weeks, not including holidays).

## MAINTENANCE LOANS FOR ENGLISH STUDENTS
## BEGINNING COURSES IN 2009/10

| Standard undergraduate course (approx. 30 weeks) | Living at parents' home | Living away from home (outside London) | Living away from home (in London) |
|---|---|---|---|
| Maintenance Loan (max) | £3,838 pa | £4,950 pa | £6,928 pa |
| 72% not means-tested | £2,763 pa | £3,564 pa | £4,988 pa |
| Remaining 28% means-tested | £1,075 pa | £1,386 pa | £1,940 pa |
| Family contribution: none expected for household income up to £50,778 | £0–1,075 pa (max. at household income of £56,153) | £0–1,386 pa (max. at household income of £57,708) | £0–1,940 pa (max. at household income of £60,478) |

## Note:

•    Family contributions are on a sliding scale with maximum amounts due at the income thresholds shown in the table. If your parents are assessed to pay the maximum contribution then their expected contribution is intended to replace all of the means-tested part of the loan. For example, if you stay in your parents' home during your studies, and your household income is £56,153 or more, you will receive only 72 per cent of the Maintenance Loan (£2,763) and your parents will be expected to contribute £1,075.

• Household income is the 'residual income' of your parents after certain allowances have been deducted, such as personal pension payments. If your parents are separated, divorced or widowed then only the income of the parent with whom you normally live will be assessed. However, if that parent has remarried, has a partner of the opposite sex or has entered into a civil partnership, both their incomes will be taken into consideration. If you qualify as an independent student (page 72), it will be your income (and that of your partner) and not your parents' income that will be used in your assessment for student funding.

• If you are eligible for a non-repayable Student Grant (page 27), this will replace part of your loan support.

• Maintenance Loan rates are lower for final year students (see www.direct.gov.uk/studentfinance) and for certain special situations, such as sandwich course students on a full year paid placement (page 80) and health profession students receiving NHS bursaries (page 89). A higher overseas rate of loan can apply for students who spend part of their course abroad (page 83).

• Maintenance Loan rates are around £200 lower for students from Wales and Northern Ireland (pages 58 and 55). For Scottish students the rates are also lower, and a higher proportion of the loan is means-tested (page 62).

## Extra Loan for longer courses

If your course year is longer than the standard 30 weeks because, for example, you have to attend a compulsory field trip at the beginning or end of term, then you may be eligible for a means-tested **Extra Loan**. The amounts range between £54 to £115 per week depending on where you are studying and whether you are living away from home.

## ● Applying for a Student Loan

Student Finance England (SFE), a new service launched by the Student Loans Company, administers Student Loans and other financial support for applicants from England and non-UK EU countries. You can apply for funding online at www.direct.gov.uk/studentfinance. This replaces the old system of applying via your Local Authority for new students.

### When to apply

Apply for a Student Loan and other government finance as soon as you can. Your money may not be available at the start of your course if you wait until you have a confirmed place. Simply quote the course that you are most likely to attend and inform Student Finance England of any changes later.

You can simplify and quicken the process by allowing UCAS to share some of the information on your application (personal details and course choice) with your student finance provider. However, the service is not available in Scotland.

### How to apply

Make sure you have a bank account set up before applying for student funding as you will need to include the bank details on the application form – otherwise your money could be delayed. Use the online Student Finance Calculator (www.direct.gov.uk/studentfinance) to work out what financial support is available to you. Then follow the stages 1–3 below to apply for any financial support that you may be entitled to – including **Student Loans, Grants** (page 26), **bursaries** (page 29) and **Supplementary Grants** such as the **Disabled Student's Allowance** (pages 75–6).

## APPLYING FOR STUDENT FUNDING

**Stage 1**

Fill in and send your application to Student Finance England (www.direct.gov.uk/ studentfinance) either online or on paper (download a paper form from the website or telephone 0845 300 50 90 for a copy). You may need to provide evidence to support your application, for example, documents confirming your household income, your country of residence and your date of birth. As part of your application, you must provide your National Insurance Number – this will be needed when you start repaying the loan at the end of your course.

**Stage 2**

Within six weeks of your application being received, it will be assessed by Student Finance England and you will be sent a Financial Notification letter. If you've applied online, you will also be sent an Online Declaration form, which you need to sign and return. You can keep track of the progress of your application by logging onto your online student finance account. Later you can manage this account online to check your payments.

**Stage 3**

Before the start of your course, Student Finance England will send you a Payment Schedule letter showing the instalments you will receive and when they are likely to be paid. You may need to show the letter to your university when you enrol.

If you are from Scotland, Wales or Northern Ireland you can also apply online through the student finance provider for your country, or download paper forms (websites on page 13). Students from non-UK countries in the EU and international students who want to study in England should turn to pages 68 and 70 respectively.

## How do you get paid?

You will normally receive your money as follows:

**GETTING MONEY INTO YOUR ACCOUNT**

| | |
|---|---|
| Stage 1 | At the beginning of term register at your university and remember to take along your Payment Schedule letter. |
| Stage 2 | Your university will confirm to Student Finance England that you are attending the course, and SFE will release the first instalment of your Maintenance Loan and any grants due to you. This money usually clears into your bank account within three to five working days so make sure you have enough to cover your first week or so at university. |
| Stage 3 | SFE will pay your Maintenance Loan and any grants in three instalments, one at the start of each term – straight into your bank or building society account. The Tuition Fee Loan will be paid directly to your university. Your university will pay you any bursary or scholarship you are entitled to. |

## ● Repaying your Student Loan

The arrangements for repaying your Student Loan are generous. You don't start repaying the loan until at least the April after you leave your course, and then only if you are in work and earning a salary of more than £15,000 (gross income, i.e. before any tax or other deductions) – equivalent to £1,250 per month or £288 per week. Thereafter, repayments will be collected from your earnings through the tax system each week or each month at the rate of 9 per cent on that part of your income over £15,000 a year. So, for example, at a salary of £20,000 before tax, your monthly repayment would be:

$$£20,000 - £15,000 = £5,000 \times 9\%$$
$$= £450 \text{ a year or } £37.50 \text{ a month}$$

Should your income fall below £15,000 (by, for example, leaving paid work to start a family or undertake voluntary work) then repayments would stop. Unlike a commercial loan, how much you repay each month is determined only by your income, not by how much you owe.

Other points to note:
•     Interest on the loan is linked to the rate of inflation and is adjusted each year.
•     The government will write off any loans outstanding after 25 years, so if by then you still haven't paid it all off, you won't have to pay the remainder (unless you have missed payments and got into arrears). In other words, most of you could taste freedom before you are 50!
•     Those of you starting repayments in 2012 or beyond will be able to take a 'repayment holiday' of up to five years but this will, of course, be added to the write-off period. This is

designed to help graduates who might need additional money to buy a house, move to a new part of the country for work, get married or start a family.

• If you want to pay off your Student Loan more quickly you can choose to make voluntary extra repayments.

**YOUR LOAN AGREEMENT**
Your Student Loan agreement is a contract and you must agree to repay your loan in line with the regulations that apply when you start making repayments. Making yourself bankrupt is not an option for clearing the debt. Nor is planning to live outside the UK following your studies: the Student Loans Company has set up separate repayment mechanisms for this situation, and it will use European Union law to enforce repayment should you default. There is more information about repaying your loan at www.studentloanrepayment.co.uk.

**Student Talk**

'You'll need to reapply for student finance each year so make sure you remember the passwords you use in your application – and reapply as early as possible.'

*The creator of Wallace and Gromit, Nick Park CBE, graduated with a degree in Fine Art from Sheffield Polytechnic (now Sheffield Hallam University).*

# 5    Student Grants

In addition to the Student Loan system, the government assists new full-time undergraduate students from less affluent homes by offering **Student Grants** (also known as '**Maintenance Grants**' and '**Special Support Grants**') to help towards your living costs at university. Unlike Student Loans, Student Grants do not have to be repaid.

➡️ **OTHER NAMES FOR STUDENT GRANTS**
Student Grants have different names in the different countries of the UK. Essentially, these grants all have the same purpose, although the amounts may differ (see chapter 8):
- England: 'Maintenance Grant' and 'Special Support Grant'
- Northern Ireland: 'Maintenance Grant'
- Wales: 'Assembly Learning Grant'
- Scotland: 'Young Students' Bursary'

## ● How much can you get?

A **Maintenance Grant** is means-tested and paid instead of part of the **Maintenance Loan** – so there will be less loan to pay off later on. Students from families with a household income of £25,000 or below receive a full Maintenance Grant of £2,906, and a reduced Maintenance Loan. (For every £1 of Maintenance Grant you receive, your Maintenance Loan entitlement is reduced by 50p.) At a household income of £50,778 or more, you receive the maximum Maintenance Loan and no Maintenance Grant. See the table for more details.

## MAINTENANCE GRANTS AND MAINTENANCE LOANS FOR ENGLISH STUDENTS BEGINNING COURSES IN 2009/10

| Household income | Maintenance Grant | Maintenance Loan (living at parents' home): max. £3,838 | Maintenance Loan (living away from home, outside London): max. £4,950 | Maintenance Loan (living away from home, In London): max. £6,928 |
| --- | --- | --- | --- | --- |
| £25,000 | £2,906 (full grant) | £2,385 | £3,497 | £5,475 |
| £40,000 | £711 (partial grant) | £3,483 | £4,595 | £6,573 |
| £50,778 | no grant | £3,838 | £4,950 | £6,928 |

You may qualify for a **Special Support Grant** if you are on Income Support or another means-tested benefit such as Housing Benefit. Your benefit entitlement will not be affected.

**HOW MANY GRANTS?**
In 2008/9 about 40 per cent of students received a full Maintenance Grant in England, and another 29 per cent received a partial grant; 31 per cent received no Maintenance Grant. The higher the grant you receive, the lower your Maintenance Loan – which means less debt to pay off after graduation. (Source: Student Loans Company Ltd, November 2008)

A Special Support Grant is paid instead of a Maintenance Grant (you don't get both). The important difference between the two types of grant is that the Special Support Grant doesn't affect how much you're entitled to through the Maintenance Loan, so with a Special Support Grant you'll be eligible for a higher Maintenance Loan.

The maximum you can get for a Special Support Grant is the same as for the Maintenance Grant (£2,906 for the academic year 2009/10). Both grants are paid by Student Finance England at the start of each term, usually directly into your bank account, along with any other payments that are due to you under the Student Loan scheme.

● **Applying for a Student Grant**
Apply using the same application form and at the same time as you apply for your Student Loan and other government funding, using either the online service provided by Student Finance England or a paper form. For more information see www.direct.gov.uk/studentfinance. Northern Irish, Scottish and Welsh students should apply to the relevant student finance provider for their country (page 13).

● **Supplementary Grants**
There are several Supplementary Grants available, for example a grant to help students with dependants, and an allowance for disabled students. More details are given in chapter 9.

## 6    Bursaries, scholarships and awards

In addition to Student Loans and Grants, the government provides extra help for students in the form of bursaries (or scholarships), which are administered by the universities themselves. Like Student Grants, bursaries do not have to be paid back. A bursary is an annual payment awarded to cover your day-to-day living costs while you are studying. It is normally paid in stages or by a lump sum. Many bursaries are means-tested and aimed at less affluent students, but some are given on the basis of academic performance or sporting or musical achievement. Others are based on certain personal circumstances, such as whether you live in a specific locality. Bursaries are also offered for particular courses, for example, **Social Work bursaries** (page 94) and **NHS bursaries** (page 89).

### ● How much can you get?

Amounts vary between universities and for different courses. If you are getting the full Maintenance Grant of £2,906 (or Special Support Grant), all publicly funded universities charging the maximum tuition fees are required to offer you at least a minimum bursary (£319 in 2009/10). In other words, your tuition fee of £3,225 is met in full by the combined total of your Maintenance Grant and the university bursary.

Universities may offer more than the minimum bursary, and many do – typical bursaries range from £319 to £3,150 for students with low household incomes.

## ● Checking what's on offer

The tables on pages 32, 44 and 46 are designed to help you compare the bursaries and scholarships on offer at institutions in England, Northern Ireland, Scotland and Wales in 2009. Additional details for some of these awards are included in Appendix 2 (page 177). Not all bursaries and scholarships are featured here and to see the full range on offer at a particular university you'll need to consult the university prospectus and/or website (see below).

**WEBLINKS TO UNIVERSITY WEBSITES**
Use the websites below to go directly to the bursary web page for a university of your choice:
- Via 'University Profiles' at www.thecompleteuniversityguide.co.uk
- Via the 'course search 2009' on the UCAS website (www.ucas.com).

## ● Bursaries to widen access to university

The current bursary system has developed out of the government's commitment to have 50 per cent of young people going into higher education by 2010. There are now more university bursaries than ever before for low-income families. These are intended to ensure that individuals are not put off coming to university through lack of funds following the introduction of university tuition fees.

Arrangements for tuition fees, bursaries and scholarships are overseen in England by the Office for Fair Access (OFFA), and in Northern Ireland by the Department for Employment and Learning. Universities have been required to submit Access Agreements outlining what fees they intend to levy and how they plan to widen access. (The nearest equivalent in Wales are the Fee Plans submitted by each university to the Higher Education Funding Council for Wales.) A significant feature of all these rather complex documents is a description of the new bursaries and scholarships on offer. Some are guaranteed and are based on your personal circumstances while others are available through open competition. It is important to read Access Agreements when you come to apply to universities as OFFA suggests that some 400,000 students are likely to benefit from these funds. The documents contain plenty of helpful information about bursaries and other funds available for would-be students. Copies of all the Access Agreements can be found on the OFFA website (www.offa.org.uk).

## BURSARY TIPS

- Check the number of bursaries on offer and be realistic about your chances. If your parents are high-income earners, then you are likely only to be eligible for those linked to your academic record or if you plan to study a 'shortage' subject.
- Read the small print. There may be lots of conditions attached.
- Look out for special (unadvertised) offers when you go to interviews and open days.
- Find out if the bursary is automatic or conditional. If it is conditional, when will you know you've got it? For means-tested bursaries, you will have a good idea of eligibility when you apply, and will know for definite when you get your student finance assessment. For others, you won't know until you receive your exam results.
- Some universities offer fee remission rather than a bursary. This is really a choice between reduced debt in the future versus cash in hand now.

## BURSARIES & SCHOLARSHIPS
ENGLAND, LATEST FIGURES PUBLISHED DEC 2008
See 'University Profiles' at www.thecompleteuniversityguide.co.uk for updates.

| Universities | Full Maintenance Grant (£) | Partial Maintenance Grant (£) | Living in region/ specified postcode | Bursaries for placement/ year abroad students |
|---|---|---|---|---|
| Anglia Ruskin | 319 + 500 pa from 2009 | | | •S |
| Arts University College Bournemouth | 350 + 175 bike voucher | 200 + 175 bike voucher | | |
| Aston | 800 min | 0–640 | | •B |
| Bath | 1,200 min | 300–900 | •B | |
| Bath Spa | 350–1,200 | up to 200 | | |
| Bedfordshire | 820 (2008–09) | 310-615 (2008–09) | | |
| Birkbeck | | | | |
| Birmingham | 860 | 860 | | |
| Birmingham City | Up to 525 (2008–09) | Up to 525 (2008–09) | | |
| Bishop Grosseteste UC | 1,075 | 1,075 | | |
| Bolton | 350 | 350 | | |
| Bournemouth | 319 | Up to 319 | | |
| Bradford | 500–900 | 400–600 | | |
| Brighton | 1,080 max | 540 min | | |
| Bristol | 1,200 | 770–310 | •B 1,075 | |
| Brunel | 1,000 | 500 | •S | |
| Buckingham | | | | |
| Buckinghamshire New | 500 | 500 | | |

B indicates where a bursary is available    MG indicates Maintenance Grant
S indicates where a scholarship is available

| Progressing from outreach | Ethnic minorities | Disabled | Sport | Care Bursary | Shortage subjects | Academic achievement |
|---|---|---|---|---|---|---|
|  |  |  | •S |  |  |  |
| •B |  |  |  | 2,000 |  | •S 150 yr 1, 250 yr 2, 500 yr 3 |
|  |  |  |  |  | •B |  |
|  |  |  | •S |  |  | •S |
|  |  |  |  |  | •S |  |
|  |  |  |  |  |  | •S |
|  |  |  |  |  |  |  |
|  |  |  |  |  | •S | •S 1,290 |
|  |  |  |  |  |  |  |
|  |  |  |  | •B 3,600 |  |  |
| •S 750 |  |  |  | •S 1,000 |  | •S 500 |
| •B 500 |  |  | •S |  |  | •S |
| •S 300 |  |  |  |  |  |  |
|  |  | •B | •S | Grant 1,000 |  | •S 1,000 |
|  |  |  | •S |  | •S | •S |
| •S | •S |  |  |  |  | •S |
|  |  |  |  |  |  |  |
| •S 300 |  |  |  |  |  |  |

BURSARIES & SCHOLARSHIPS – **ENGLAND**

| Universities | Full Maintenance Grant (£) | Partial Maintenance Grant (£) | Living in region/ specified postcode | Bursaries for placement/ year abroad students |
|---|---|---|---|---|
| Cambridge | 3,250 | 50–2,000 | •B | |
| Canterbury Christ Church | 860 | 535 | | |
| Central Lancashire | 500 | 500 | •B | •B |
| Central School of Speech and Drama | 500 | | | |
| Chester | 1,000 | | | |
| Chichester | 1,077 | 0–1,026 | | |
| City | 750 | 350 | •S | |
| Courtauld Institute of Art | 319 | 319 | | |
| Coventry | 320 | 320 | | |
| Creative Arts | 319 | | | |
| Cumbria | 1,290 | 215–1,070 | •S | |
| De Montfort | 500 | 500 | •B 250 | |
| Derby | 830 | up to 520 | •B 300 | |
| Durham | 1,300 | 525 or 750 | | |
| East Anglia | 600 | 300 | | |
| East London | 319 | | | |
| Edge Hill | 500 | | | |

| Progressing from outreach | Ethnic minorities | Disabled | Sport | Care Bursary | Shortage subjects | Academic achievement |
|---|---|---|---|---|---|---|
| | | •B | | | | |
| | | | •S | | | |
| •B | | | •S 4,000 | | •S | •S 2,000 |
| | | | | | | |
| | | | | | | |
| | | | | | | |
| | | | | | •S | |
| •S | | | | | | |
| •S 1,000 | | | •S 1,000– 4,000 | | •S 3,225 | •S 2,000 |
| | | | | | | •S |
| •S | | •S | | | | •S |
| •S 1,000 | | | | •B 1,000 | | •S 1,000 |
| •B 400 | | | | | | |
| | | | •S 3,000 | | | •S 3,000 |
| | | | •S 1,000 | | | •S 500–4,000 |
| | | | •S 1,000 | | | •S 1,000 |
| | | | •S 2,000 | •B | | •S 2,000 |

## BURSARIES & SCHOLARSHIPS – **ENGLAND**

| Universities | Full Maintenance Grant (£) | Partial Maintenance Grant (£) | Living in region/ specified postcode | Bursaries for placement/ year abroad students |
|---|---|---|---|---|
| Essex | 319 | Sliding scale | | |
| Exeter | 1,500 | 750 | •B | |
| Gloucestershire | 319 | | •B | |
| Goldsmiths, University of London | 1,000 max | Up to 500 | •S | |
| Greenwich* | n/a | n/a | | |
| Harper Adams UC | 1,000 | Up to 750 | | |
| Hertfordshire | 1,000 | | | |
| Heythrop | 50% MG | 50% MG | | |
| Huddersfield | 500 | | | |
| Hull | 1,000 | 500–1,000 | •B | |
| Imperial College London | 3,000 | Up to 2,000 | | |
| Keele | 319/800 | | | •B |
| Kent | 1,000 | 250–1,000 | | |
| King's College London | 1,350 | Up to 1,050 | | |
| Kingston | 310–1,000 | 310–1,000 | | |
| Lancaster | 1,315 | 0–500 | | |
| Leeds | 1,540 | Up to 1,335 | •S | |
| Leeds Metropolitan* | n/a | n/a | | |
| Leicester | 1,019–1,319 | Up to 400 | | |
| Lincoln | 600 | Sliding scale based on level of MG | | |
| Liverpool | 1,400 | | •B | |

*Greenwich will charge a tuition fee of £2,900 in 2009 rather than the full £3,225
*Leeds Metropolitan will charge a tuition fee of £2,000 in 2009 rather than the full £3,225

| Progressing from outreach | Ethnic minorities | Disabled | Sport | Care Bursary | Shortage subjects | Academic achievement |
|---|---|---|---|---|---|---|
| | | | •S | | •S | |
| •B | | | •S 1,000 | | •S 3,000 | •S 5,000 |
| •B | | | | •S | | •S |
| •S | | | | | | •S 500–5,000 |
| •B | | | | •B | | •S 500 |
| | | | | | | •S 1,000 |
| | | | | | •S | •S |
| | | | | | | |
| | | | | | | |
| | | | | | | •S 3,000 |
| | | | •S | | | •S 4,000 |
| •B | | | | •B | | •S 1,000 |
| •S | | | •S | | | •S |
| | | | | | | •S 1,800 |
| •B | | | | | | |
| | | | | | | •S |
| •S | | | | | | |
| | | | •S | | | |
| | | | | | | •S 1,000 |
| | | | | | | |
| | | | •S | | •S 1,500 | •B •S |

## BURSARIES & SCHOLARSHIPS – **ENGLAND**

| Universities | Full Maintenance Grant (£) | Partial Maintenance Grant (£) | Living in region/ specified postcode | Bursaries for placement/ year abroad students |
|---|---|---|---|---|
| Liverpool Hope | 500 | 500 | •S | |
| Liverpool John Moores | 1,075 | 430 | | |
| London Metropolitan | Up to 1,000 | Up to 775 | | |
| London School of Economics | 2,500 | Up to 2,500 | | |
| London South Bank | 319 | | | |
| Loughborough | 1,360 | 630 | | |
| Manchester | 1,250 | | •S | |
| Manchester Metropolitan | 1,025 | 475 | | |
| Middlesex | 319 | | •S | |
| Newcastle | 1,280 | 640 | | |
| Newman | Up to 1,100 (2008) | Up to 500 (2008) | | |
| Northampton | 1,000 | 500–700 | •B | |
| Northumbria | 319 | | •B •S | |
| Norwich University College of the Arts | 800 | 300 | | |
| Nottingham | 1,080 | 270–1,080 | •B | |
| Nottingham Trent | 1,075 | 360–665 | •B | |
| Open University | | | | |
| Oxford | 3,225 | 200–3,225 | | |
| Oxford Brookes | 1,560-1,800 | sliding scale | | |
| Plymouth | 1,015 | 300 | •B | |
| Portsmouth | 900 | Up to 600 | | |

| Progressing from outreach | Ethnic minorities | Disabled | Sport | Care Bursary | Shortage subjects | Academic achievement |
|---|---|---|---|---|---|---|
| •S | | | •S | | | •S |
| •S | | | •S | | | •S |
| | | | | | | •S |
| | | | | | | |
| | | | | | | |
| | | | | | •S | •S |
| | | | | | •S | •S |
| | | | | | | |
| | | | •S | | | •S |
| •S | | | •B | | | •S |
| | | | | | | |
| | | | | | | |
| | •S | •S | | | | |
| | | | | | | |
| •B | | | | | •B | |
| | | | | | | •S |
| | | | | | | |
| | | | | | | •B •S |
| •S 1,000 | | | | | | •S 2,000 |
| •B | | | | •B | •B | •S |
| •B | | | | •B | | |

## BURSARIES & SCHOLARSHIPS - **ENGLAND**

| Universities | Full Maintenance Grant (£) | Partial Maintenance Grant (£) | Living in region/ specified postcode | Bursaries for placement/ year abroad students |
|---|---|---|---|---|
| Queen Mary, University of London | 1,078 | 861 | •B | |
| Reading | 1,400 | 470–940 | | |
| Roehampton | 500 | | | |
| Royal Academy of Music | 600 | Up to 400 | | |
| Royal Agricultural College | 1615 + 500 | Up to 1,025 | | |
| Royal College of Music | 1,000 | Up to 1,000 | | |
| Royal Holloway | 750 | Up to 750 | | |
| Royal Northern College of Music | 1,050 | 310–1050 | | |
| Royal Veterinary College | 1,650 | Up to 1,082 | | |
| Salford | 319 | | •B | •S 1,000 |
| School of Pharmacy | 500 | 100–400 | | |
| Sheffield | 700 | 430 | | |
| Sheffield Hallam | 700 | | | |
| SOAS | 860 | 420 | | |
| Southampton | 1,000 | 500 | •B | |
| Southampton Solent | 1,075 | 250–750 | •S | |
| St George's Hospital Medical School | 1,295 | Up to 865 | | |
| St Mary's, Twickenham | 500 | 500 | | |
| St Mary's UC | 500 | 500 | | |
| Staffordshire | 1,000 | 500–1,000 | | |

| Progressing from outreach | Ethnic minorities | Disabled | Sport | Care Bursary | Shortage subjects | Academic achievement |
|---|---|---|---|---|---|---|
|  |  |  |  |  |  |  |
| •B |  |  |  |  |  |  |
|  |  |  | •S |  |  | •S 1,000 |
|  |  |  |  |  |  |  |
|  |  |  |  |  |  |  |
|  |  |  | •S |  |  | •S |
|  |  |  |  |  |  | •S |
|  |  |  | •S |  |  | •S 500 |
|  |  |  |  |  |  | •S |
|  |  |  |  |  |  | •S |
|  |  |  |  |  | •S 1,000 | •S 1,000 |
|  |  |  |  |  |  | •B |
| •B |  |  | •B |  | •B | •B |
| •B |  |  |  | •B |  | •S |
| •B 800 |  |  |  |  |  |  |
| •B |  |  |  |  |  | •S |
| •S |  |  |  |  |  |  |
|  |  |  |  |  |  |  |
|  |  |  |  |  |  |  |
|  |  |  | •S |  |  |  |
|  |  |  |  |  |  |  |

## BURSARIES & SCHOLARSHIPS – **ENGLAND**

| Universities | Full Maintenance Grant (£) | Partial Maintenance Grant (£) | Living in region/ specified postcode | Bursaries for placement/ year abroad students |
|---|---|---|---|---|
| Sunderland | 525 | 525 | | |
| Surrey | Up to 2,050 | Sliding scale | •S | |
| Sussex | 1,000 | | •S | |
| Teesside | 1,025 | | | |
| Thames Valley | 1,060 | 530 discretionary | | |
| University of the Arts, London | 319 | 1,000 discretionary | •B | |
| University College Birmingham | 1,080 | 324–648 | | |
| University for the Creative Arts | 319 | | | |
| University College Falmouth | 850 | 325–500 | | |
| University College London | 1,550–2,775 | 50% of MG value | | |
| UC Plymouth St Mark and St John | 319 | | | |
| Warwick | 1,800 | Up to 1,800 | | |
| UWE Bristol | 1,000 | | | |
| Westminster | 319 | 319 | | |
| Winchester | 820 | 410 | | |
| Wolverhampton | 500 | 300 | | |
| Worcester | 750 | 625 | | |
| York | 1,400 | Up to 1,400 | | |
| York St John | 540–1,610 on a sliding scale | | | |

| Progressing from outreach | Ethnic minorities | Disabled | Sport | Care Bursary | Shortage subjects | Academic achievement |
|---|---|---|---|---|---|---|
| | | | | | | •B |
| | | | | •S | •S | •S |
| | •S | | | | | |
| | | | | •B | •S | •S |
| | | | | | | |
| | | | | | | |
| | | | | | | |
| | | | | | | |
| | | | | •B | | |
| | | | | | | |
| | | | | | | |
| | | | | | | •S |
| •B | | | | •B | | |
| | | •S | | | | •S |
| •S | | | | •S | | •S |
| | | | •S | | | •S |
| | | | •S | | | •S |
| | | | | | | |
| | | | | | | |

**BURSARIES & SCHOLARSHIPS**
**NORTHERN IRELAND**, LATEST FIGURES PUBLISHED DEC 2008

| Universities | Full Maintenance Grant (£) | Partial Maintenance Grant (£) | Living in region/ specified postcode | Bursaries for placement/ year abroad students |
|---|---|---|---|---|
| Queen's Belfast | 1,050 | 0–530 | | |
| Ulster | 1,040 | 310–620 | | |

See 'University Profiles' at www.thecompleteuniversityguide.co.uk for updates.

**BURSARIES & SCHOLARSHIPS**
**WALES**, LATEST FIGURES PUBLISHED DEC 2008

| Universities | Full Maintenance Grant (£) | Partial Maintenance Grant (£) | Living in region/ specified postcode | Bursaries for placement/ year abroad students |
|---|---|---|---|---|
| Aberystwyth | | | | |
| Bangor | 1,000 | 500 | •S | |
| Cardiff | 1,050 | 500 | | |
| Cardiff Institute, UWIC | Up to 500 | Up to 300 | | |
| Glamorgan | 319 | | •S | |
| Glyndwr | 1,000 | 500–750 | | |
| Lampeter | 305 | | | |
| Newport | 1,000 | Up to 600 | •S | |
| Swansea | 319 | | | |
| Swansea Metropolitan | | | | |

B indicates where a bursary is available
S indicates where a scholarship is available

| Progressing from outreach | Ethnic minorities | Disabled | Sport | Care Bursary | Shortage subjects | Academic achievement |
|---|---|---|---|---|---|---|
| | | | | | | |
| | | | | | | |

B indicates where a bursary is available
S indicates where a scholarship is available

| Progressing from outreach | Ethnic minorities | Disabled | Sport | Care Bursary | Shortage subjects | Academic achievement |
|---|---|---|---|---|---|---|
| | | | •B | | •S | •S |
| | | | •S | •B 1,000 | •S | •S |
| | | | | | | •S |
| | | | •S | •B | | •S |
| •S | | | •S | | | •S |
| | | | •S | •S | | •S |
| | | | | | | •S |
| | | | | | | |
| | | | | | | |
| | | | | | | |

## BURSARIES & SCHOLARSHIPS
### SCOTLAND, LATEST FIGURES PUBLISHED DEC 2008
See 'University Profiles' at www.thecompleteuniversityguide.co.uk for updates.

| Universities | Full Maintenance Grant (£) | Partial Maintenance Grant (£) | Living in region/ specified postcode | Bursaries for placement/ year abroad students |
|---|---|---|---|---|
| Aberdeen | 310* | | •S | |
| Abertay Dundee | 310* | | | |
| Dundee | 310* | | | |
| Edinburgh | 310* (180 Entrance Bursaries of 1,000–2,500) | | | |
| Edinburgh Napier | 310* | | | |
| Glasgow | 310* | | | |
| Glasgow Caledonian | 310* | | | |
| Heriot-Watt | 310* | | | |
| Queen Margaret UC | 310* | | | |
| Robert Gordon | 310* | | | |
| Royal Scottish Academy of Music and Drama | 310* | | | |
| St Andrews | 310* | | | |
| Stirling | 310* | | | |
| Strathclyde | 310* | | | |
| UHI Millennium Institute | 310* | | | |
| West of Scotland | 310* | | | |

* The RUK (rest of UK) Bursary has been introduced for students normally resident in England, Wales or Northern Ireland only, studying at a Scottish university, who would otherwise have been eligible for a £319 national minimum bursary (i.e. in receipt of full MG) had they studied at a university in the rest of the UK. The RUK Bursary is currently worth around £310.

B indicates where a bursary is available        MG indicates Maintenance Grant
S indicates where a scholarship is available

| Progressing from outreach | Ethnic minorities | Disabled | Sport | Care Bursary | Shortage subjects | Academic achievement |
|---|---|---|---|---|---|---|
|  |  |  |  |  |  | •S |
|  |  |  |  | •grant |  |  |
|  |  |  |  |  |  | •S |
|  |  |  | •B |  | •S |  |
|  |  |  |  |  |  |  |
| •B |  |  |  |  |  | •S 1,000 |
|  |  |  | •S |  | •S | •S |
|  |  |  | •S |  | •S |  |
|  |  |  |  |  |  |  |
|  |  |  | •S |  |  | •S |
|  |  |  |  |  |  |  |
|  |  |  |  |  | •S |  |
|  |  | •S | •S |  |  |  |
|  |  |  | •B |  |  |  |
|  |  |  |  |  |  |  |
|  |  |  |  |  |  |  |
|  |  |  |  |  |  |  |

● **How to apply**

Check with the individual universities as they set their own procedures for applications. A number of universities are quite specific about application procedures and indicate both the timing and availability of online applications, including a timetable for notification of decisions. Some universities have gone out of their way to keep things simple and will not require an application at all; entitlement will be calculated automatically when your student finance application is assessed without you having to do anything else.

For most bursaries you will need to reapply each year and the eligibility criteria may change in your second year. For example, a means-tested award in year one may only be available based on performance in year two.

● **When do you get paid?**

Payment of bursaries from some universities is through Student Finance England while others administer their schemes in-house. Check with the Access Agreement (page 31) and the university about whether the bursary will be paid at the beginning of the academic year or as staged payments during the year. Some bursaries are a combination of cash and a discounted service, for example, discounted accommodation or entrance to sports facilities.

● **Special circumstances**

If your personal circumstances change part-way through the course, for example, through unsatisfactory academic progress or a change in family income, then your entitlement

**Student Talk**

*'I did apply for a bursary, and I should have received it as I fitted the criteria, but unfortunately, I missed the deadline and so had to be turned down. My advice is to start looking early for anything you might be entitled to, and apply straight away. Don't put it to one side and promise to fill it in tomorrow, because you'll probably forget all about it.'*

will be reviewed. If you spend time abroad, on a placement or as part of a sandwich degree, reduced tuition fees and bursaries will normally apply. Foundation year studies also often attract lower fees and/or bursaries.

## ● Other awards

Some charities, educational trusts and professional bodies may be willing to award a bursary or scholarship. The amounts can vary from a one-off payment of a few pounds to pay for some books or equipment, to several thousands given each year for the duration of your course to cover living costs. Be realistic about your chances as competition is keen and financial help through these means is very difficult to come by. Many charities and trusts will only consider giving support once you have exhausted the government funding options available, such as **Student Loans** and **Hardship Funds** (page 52).

Here are a few examples of the charities, trusts and professional institutions you might consider:

• Charities such as Scope (a UK disability organisation whose focus is people with cerebral palsy; www.scope.org.uk) and the Royal National Institute for Blind People (RNIB; www.rnib.org.uk) offer help in various forms for students with disabilities.

• The Honourable Society of Gray's Inn (www.graysinn. org.uk) helps people studying law; the Worshipful Company of Chartered Surveyors (www.surveyorslivery. org.uk) helps those studying Surveying. See also the professional institutions below.

• Some trusts are set up to help children of parents in a particular profession. For example, The Royal Medical Benevolent Fund (www.rmbf.org) helps children of medical graduates.

• There are also local trusts that offer help depending on where you live.

• Some professional institutions offer scholarships and awards to encourage people to take up a particular career. For example, the Institution of Engineering and Technology (IET) offers scholarships in engineering as there is a global shortage of engineers. The awards of up to £3,000 per annum are to help you finance your studies at a university in the UK or Ireland, and there may be help with travel costs on top. The course must be IET accredited. Applications are accepted on the basis of financial need (you'll also need Bs at A level to be eligible) and/or academic excellence (for example, 3 As at A level). You'll need a reference from your school or college tutor or employer confirming your academic ability. An IET award can be held in addition to a Student Loan, grant and any company support. For more information, go to www.theiet.org/education. For similar awards try:

– The Institution of Mechanical Engineers, www.imeche.org

– The Institution of Civil Engineers, www.ice.org.uk/quest
– The Institute of Marine Engineering, Science and Technology, www.imarest.org

## ● Further information

• Ask your school or Local Authority for a list of local charities that offer help to students in higher education.

• The Education Grants Advisory Service (EGAS) advises students on which organisations to contact for financial aid. Fill in the online educational grants search on their website (www.family-action.org.uk/section.aspx?id=1037) to identify trusts that may be able to assist you. Besides representing a wide range of individual trusts and charities, EGAS also administers over 30 educational trusts themselves, giving small grants primarily to students who study at institutions that are affiliated to their service.

• Consult the *The Educational Grants Directory* published by the Directory of Social Change – this is expensive so try your local reference library.

➡ **YOUR STUDENT LOAN ENTITLEMENT**
Awards from charities and trusts are not usually taken into account in the government's calculation of your Student Loan, Grant, etc.

## 7 Hardship (Access) Funds

The **Access to Learning Fund** is a further source of modest government help to students in financial difficulties and is allocated by the universities themselves. This can provide help with day-to-day study and living costs for students who might otherwise have to leave their course because of financial problems, or emergency payments for an unexpected crisis. The university decides which students need support and the level of support it will offer. Money is normally given as a grant, which you don't need to pay back, although sometimes you may receive a short-term loan. Similar help is available from universities in Scotland, Wales and Northern Ireland – for more details check with your university or student finance provider.

### ● Who is eligible?

Full-time undergraduate 'home' students (ordinarily resident in the UK) and part-time students if their courses last at least one year and take no more than twice as long to complete as an equivalent full-time course. The university will look at your individual circumstances to assess your level of need. Priority is given to students with children, mature students, students from low-income families, those who are homeless or in sheltered accommodation, final-year students and disabled students.

**NAMES FOR HARDSHIP FUNDS**

There are different names for Hardship Funds in each country of the UK:

- England – 'Access to Learning Fund'
- Northern Ireland – 'Support Funds'
- Scotland – 'Discretionary Fund'
- Wales – 'Financial Contingency Fund'

## How much do you get?

Hardship funding is discretionary and the amounts awarded vary considerably. You may get £200 to help pay a bill, or several thousand pounds if you can't pay the rent and there's no one else to turn to. The amount also depends on how much is left in the fund for the year – make sure you apply early to get ahead in the queue. The university will decide whether to pay you in a lump sum or instalments. Money from the Access to Learning Fund is paid on top of your standard student finance package – it is not meant as a substitute.

## How to apply

Each institution has its own procedure but the normal method is to apply through the Student Services department at your university once you've started your course and after you've received your Student Loan, Grant, etc. By then you'll have a fair idea how quickly your money is being used up and what extra help you will need. Bear in mind that it can take several weeks to assess your application so don't hang about if you see financial trouble looming. You may need to supply a letter confirming your finance award from your student finance provider and bank statements and other documents showing your financial situation. You can apply more than once in a year.

● **Other Hardship Funds**

•    Some universities have additional resources to help students who are suffering financially, perhaps because of a death or a family illness. Some of this money may come from fundraising groups or external charitable trusts; some is administered through the Students' Union. Check with the Student Services department.

•    The Foyer-UNIAID Accommodation Bursary gives one year's free or supported accommodation to full-time 'home' students on undergraduate courses in the UK who are at risk of having to leave university because of extreme hardship. You have to be studying in one of the cities where they operate – see the terms and conditions and apply online at www.uniaid. org.uk/bursaries.

# 8 Geographical differences

So far we've covered the main principles of UK student funding and in particular the arrangements for England. It's now time to look at the figures for Northern Ireland, Wales and Scotland (the table on the next page provides a summary of the arrangements for all the UK countries). In this chapter you'll also find information on funding for EU and International students.

## ● Northern Ireland

The student support system in Northern Ireland is very similar to that in England. The maximum tuition fees charged in 2009/10 are the same as in England (£3,225) and you can apply for a **Tuition Fee Loan** (page 16) to cover your tuition fee in full. The **Maintenance Loan** rates are slightly lower, with maximum levels as follows:

**MAINTENANCE LOAN FOR NORTHERN IRISH STUDENTS BEGINNING THEIR STUDIES IN 2009/10**

|  | Living at parents' home | Living away from home (outside London) | Living away from home (in London) |
|---|---|---|---|
| Maintenance Loan (max.) – standard 30-week course | £3,673 | £4,745 | £6,643 |

## STUDENT FINANCE ARRANGEMENTS AVAILABLE
## IN EACH UK COUNTRY, 2009/10

|  | Students living in | | | |
|---|---|---|---|---|
|  | England | Northern Ireland | Wales | Scotland |
| Pay tuition fees themselves | Yes | Yes | Yes | No (if staying in Scotland) |
| Tuition Fee Loan | Yes | Yes | Yes | Yes (if not staying in Scotland) |
| Maintenance Loan | Yes | Yes | Yes | Yes |
| Maintenance Grant | Yes | Yes | No | No |
| Assembly Learning Grant | No | No | Yes | No |
| Welsh Bursary Scheme | Yes (if going to Wales) | Yes (if going to Wales) | Yes (if staying in Wales) | Yes (if going to Wales) |
| University Bursary (statutory) | Yes | Yes | Yes | Yes (if not staying in Scotland) |
| Young Students' Bursary | No | No | No | Yes (if staying in Scotland) |
| Additional Loan (Scotland) | No | No | No | Yes (if staying in Scotland) |
| Students Outside Scotland Bursary | No | No | No | Yes (if not staying in Scotland) |

As in England, there is a means-tested **Extra Loan** for courses that are longer than the standard 30 weeks. For example, for each extra week you live away from home (in London) you may be eligible for a maximum of £106 per week, living elsewhere you may get up to £83 per week, and living at home a maximum of £54 a week.

The means-tested **Maintenance Grant** (and the **Special Support Grant**) is £500 higher than for England (page 27) but the household income cut-off point for receiving the grant is lower.

**MAINTENANCE GRANT FOR NORTHERN IRISH STUDENTS BEGINNING THEIR STUDIES IN 2009/10**

| Household income 2009/10 | How much you get |
|---|---|
| £18,820 pa or less | Full grant: £3,406 |
| Between £18,821 and £40,238 pa | Partial grant |
| Over £40,238 pa | No grant |

As in England, the Maintenance Grant and Special Support Grant do not need to be repaid. Up to £1,792 of the Maintenance Grant is paid in substitution for an element of the Maintenance Loan, so that your Maintenance Loan is reduced by up to the amount of Maintenance Grant you are paid.

The **bursary** system is essentially the same as in England (page 29). Universities charging full tuition fees are required to provide extra financial help for students who are entitled to the full Maintenance Grant or Special Support Grant, and you may also get a bursary if you receive a partial grant. Contact the universities you are interested in to find out what's on offer.

**Access to Learning Funds** (known as **Support Funds** in Northern Irish institutions) are available through your university and provide extra funding for students who need financial help in order to stay at university. As in England, these are usually paid as grants and do not have to be repaid, although sometimes they can be given as short-term loans. Your university or college will decide whether to pay you in a lump sum or in instalments.

There are also **Supplementary Grants** for students with dependants, and for disabled students – see pages 74 and 75.

## How to apply

If your home is in Northern Ireland and you plan to study at a university in the UK, you can make an online application for student funding to Student Finance Northern Ireland (www.studentfinanceni.co.uk). The website includes an online calculator which will estimate your financial support for courses starting in 2009/10. Students can also apply for student funding through their Education and Library Board (ELB). If you are planning to study in Northern Ireland but normally live in another country in the UK, then apply to the student finance provider for your country. Students from other countries in the EU or outside the EU who want to study in Northern Ireland should turn to pages 68–71.

## ● Wales

The Welsh Assembly has determined its own rules and regulations for student funding. Universities in Wales can charge their own level of fees, up to a limit of £3,225 for the academic year 2009/10, but they can also reduce the fees especially for Welsh students.

## a) Welsh students studying in Wales

Welsh students who choose to study in Wales receive a **Tuition Fee Grant** of £1,940 irrespective of household income, and this doesn't have to be repaid. Under EU law, this also applies to EU students not from the UK. In effect this reduces the tuition fees paid by Welsh students at Welsh universities to £1,285 per year (£3,225 minus £1,940). You can apply to Student Finance Wales for a **Tuition Fee Loan** to cover your reduced fees.

Welsh students (but not EU students from other countries this time) can also apply for a **Maintenance Loan** to cover living costs. The loan rates are slightly lower than in England:

### MAINTENANCE LOAN FOR WELSH STUDENTS BEGINNING COURSES IN 2009/10

|  | Living at parents' home | Living away from home (outside London) | Living away from home (in London) |
|---|---|---|---|
| Maintenance Loan (max.) – standard 30-week course | £3,673 | £4,745 | £6,648 |

On top of your Maintenance Loan you may get a means-tested **Extra Loan** if your course is longer than the standard 30 weeks – similar to the extra loan amounts available through the English system. This amounts to a maximum of £55 per week extra if you live with your parents, £83 per week if you live away from home (but not in London), and £106 per week if you live away from home in London.

If you normally live in Wales you may also be eligible for an **Assembly Learning Grant** (ALG) to help with living costs. Like the English Maintenance Grant, this is means-tested but the income threshold is much lower (you receive no grant if your household income is over £39,329 per annum). The table below shows how much you could get:

**ASSEMBLY LEARNING GRANT FOR 2009/10**

| Household income | Assembly Learning Grant (ALG) |
|---|---|
| £0–£18,370 pa | £2,906 |
| £18,371–£39,329 pa | Partial grant |
| Over £39,329 pa | No grant |

Your repayable Maintenance Loan will be reduced by the amount you receive in non-repayable Assembly Learning Grant, up to £1,288.

**NEW WELSH RULES FROM 2010**
The Tuition Fee Grant is to be phased out in 2010. It will not be available for Welsh (or EU) students who begin their studies in Wales in 2010. However, the means-tested Assembly Learning Grant for some of these students will be increased from £2,906 to £5,000 to help with living costs. Students beginning courses before 2010 will continue to be entitled to the Tuition Fee Grant until they finish their degree.

**Hardship Funds** in Wales are known as **Financial Contingency Funds** and these are available through your university. You can apply if you are experiencing financial difficulties.

Under the Welsh Bursary Scheme, if you are a new full-time student beginning an undergraduate course in Wales, regardless of where you come from in the UK, you will be considered for a means-tested **Welsh National Bursary**. The amount is £319 a year. You will be automatically assessed for this bursary when you apply for your student finance package. Universities and colleges may offer other **bursaries** and **scholarships** at their discretion (page 44). Check directly with the universities you are interested in.

There are also **Supplementary Grants** for students with dependants and for disabled students – see pages 74 and 75.

## How to apply

For your main student finance package, apply to Student Finance Wales (www.studentfinancewales.co.uk). For an Assembly Learning Grant, apply to your Local Authority – you can download an application form at www.studentfinance-wales.co.uk.

## b) Welsh students studying outside Wales

If you normally live in Wales but decide to study in England or Northern Ireland, you are not entitled to the Tuition Fee Grant and you will be liable for the full fees charged by the university you have chosen, up to a maximum of £3,225. However, if you decide to study in Scotland you will be charged a tuition fee of only £1,820 a year (or £1,285 for some degrees), except Medicine which incurs a fee of £2,895 a year. You can apply to Student Finance Wales for a **Tuition Fee Loan** to cover your fees in full in each case, and for a **Maintenance Loan**. You can also apply to your Local Authority for a means-tested **Assembly Learning Grant**, as above. Additionally, there may be a **bursary** or **scholarship** for which you are eligible at your chosen university (pages 33–7), and **Supplementary Grants** (pages 74 and 75).

## How to apply

Apply in the same way as above for Welsh students studying in Wales.

### c) English, Scottish and Northern Irish students studying in Wales

You will pay tuition fees to Welsh universities of up to £3,225. You can apply for a **Tuition Fee Loan** (page 16), a **Maintenance Loan** (page 17) and a **Maintenance Grant** (page 18) from the student finance provider for your country (for example, Student Finance England). You may also be eligible for a **Welsh National Bursary** and any other bursaries given by Welsh universities (page 44).

## How to apply

For your main student finance package (Tuition Fee Loan, Maintenance Loan and Maintenance Grant) contact the student finance provider for your country – page 13.

● **Scotland**

Soon after the Scottish Parliament was set up in 1998, it took its own independent line on student funding arrangements and, in particular, on university tuition fees. There are now considerable differences between the Scottish and English systems (see the table at the beginning of this chapter, page 56). For more details check the Student Awards Agency for Scotland (SAAS) website (www.saas.gov.uk).

The funds available to you will depend on whether you plan to study in Scotland or elsewhere in the UK.

## a) Scottish students studying in Scotland

Provided you satisfy the residency requirements (your normal home is in Scotland), you will pay no tuition fee to study at a Scottish university (this also applies to non-UK EU students). So you won't need a Tuition Fee Loan. However, you do still need to apply to the SAAS to have your tuition fee paid for you each academic year – the SAAS pays the fees straight to your university or college.

The means-tested **Maintenance Loan** rates are a little lower than in England: the maximum rate for a full-time, standard 30-week academic year if you are living in Scotland but away from home is £4,625 (see the table overleaf). You can apply for the maximum loan if your household income is below £24,275 (£20,645 if you are an independent student and the income of your spouse, civil partner or partner is to be assessed instead of that of your parents). Family contributions are on a sliding scale with the maximum amounts due at the income thresholds shown in the table. For example, if you are living away from your parents' home (but not in London) and your household

➡ **SCOTTISH PARENTAL CONTRIBUTIONS**
Scottish parents have an obligation to support their children (aged over 18 and up to 25) while at university. As in England, your parents' contribution is treated as part of your support, and the amount you receive in student funding is reduced by the amount of their assessed contribution. A family with a household income below £24,275 is not expected to contribute. Wealthier Scottish families may find themselves expected to contribute more than in the English system, but then Scottish students studying in Scotland are favoured by less debt through the policy of no tuition fees.

income is over £55,804, you will receive only the minimum (non means-tested part of the) loan – i.e. £915 – and your parents will be expected to contribute £3,710.

## MAINTENANCE LOAN FOR SCOTTISH STUDENTS BEGINNING COURSES IN 2009/10

|  | Living at home | Living away from home (outside London) | Living away from home (in London) |
|---|---|---|---|
| Maintenance Loan (max.) – standard 30-week course | £3,665 | £4,625 | £5,710 |
| 16–20% not means-tested | £605 pa | £915 pa | £915 pa |
| Remaining 80–84% means-tested | £3,060 pa | £3,710 pa | £4,795 pa |
| Family contribution: none expected for household income up to £24,275 | £1–3,060 pa (max. at household income of £51,579) | £1–3,710 pa (max. at household income of £55,804) | £1–4,795 pa (max. at household income of £62,856) |

## Note:

• If your course is longer than the standard 30 weeks you can apply for an additional means-tested **Extra Loan** – maximum weekly payments of £54 if you are living in your parents' home and £83 if you are living elsewhere.

• If you are eligible for the non-repayable **Young Students' Bursary** (see opposite), this will replace part of your loan support.

Scottish students (and non-UK EU students) studying full-time on undergraduate courses in Scotland may also be eligible for a **Young Students' Bursary** to help with living costs (this is similar to the Maintenance Grant in England). Aimed at students from lower-income families, the Young Students' Bursary (which is only available if you are under 25 at the beginning of your course) doesn't need to be paid back. It replaces part of your Maintenance Loan and so reduces the amount of loan you need to take out.

## YOUNG STUDENTS' BURSARY FOR STUDENTS BEGINNING COURSES IN 2009/10

| Household income | How much you get |
| --- | --- |
| £19,310 pa or less | Full bursary: £2,640 |
| £23,000 pa | Partial bursary: £1,986 |
| Over £34,195 pa | No bursary |

The bursary is a maximum of £2,640 for a household income of £19,310 or less and reduces on a sliding scale down to zero for a household income over £34,195 a year. When the bursary level reduces to zero, your living cost support is entirely through your Maintenance Loan and your parents' contribution. Check the SAAS website for eligibility criteria and further details.

If you are eligible for a Young Students' Bursary, you may also be eligible for a means-tested **Additional Loan**: up to £605 for a household income of £17,835 or less a year, down to zero for a household income over £21,760 a year.

A means-tested **Travel Expenses Grant** is available for students from families with low incomes to help towards daily travel costs and visits home. If you are living at home this can be over £800 a year for a standard course (academic year of approximately 30 weeks) or around £500 if you live away from home.

You can also apply to individual universities in Scotland for **Hardship Funds** (known as **Discretionary Funds** in Scotland). The universities use these funds to provide scholarships or bursaries, giving priority to students who otherwise may not have come to university because of their financial circumstances. Check the university websites and prospectuses for details, or enquire with the Student Services department at the university where you wish to apply. A useful online map linking you to the relevant financial web pages for Scottish universities is at: www.saas.gov.uk/institutions_map.htm.

There are also **Supplementary Grants** for lone parents, students with dependants, students leaving care to enter higher education, and students with disabilities – see the SAAS website for details.

### How to apply

Students from Scotland and non-UK EU countries may apply online for their main student finance package through the SAAS website (www.saas.gov.uk).

### b) Scottish students studying outside Scotland

You will pay the same tuition fees to your university as English students (up to £3,225 each year). Apply to SAAS for a **Tuition Fee Loan**, and remember to apply each year of your course as SAAS does not pay the fees automatically. The Tuition Fee Loan is not means-tested – everyone is entitled to a loan for the full amount.

You are eligible for the **Maintenance Loan** at the same rates as Scottish students studying in Scotland, although there is a higher rate if you live and study in London (page 64). You can also get a means-tested **Extra Loan** if your course is longer than the standard 30 weeks. If you live away from home in London, this can be up to £106 per week on top of the standard loan, or £83 per week for elsewhere in the UK.

In addition you may be eligible for a means-tested **Students' Outside Scotland Bursary**, which is paid instead of part of the means-tested Maintenance Loan and is similar to the Young Students' Bursary available to students studying in Scotland (and the Maintenance Grant in England). The Students' Outside Scotland Bursary is available to both young and mature students studying at UK institutions outside Scotland. The maximum is slightly lower than the Young Students' Bursary, at £2,150 a year for a household income of £19,310.

An **Additional Loan** and a **Travel Expenses Grant** are also available, depending on your household income – the rates are the same as for Scottish students studying in Scotland (pages 65–6). You can apply for **Supplementary Grants** in the same way as students staying in Scotland. If you experience financial difficulties while at university you can apply for **Discretionary Funds** (page 52) or other **Hardship Funds** at the university at which you are studying.

## How to apply

For your main student finance package, apply to SAAS (www.saas.gov.uk) as any other Scottish student.

## (c) English, Welsh and Northern Irish students studying in Scotland

If you are ordinarily resident in England, Wales or Northern Ireland, you will have to pay tuition fees for each year of your course if you want to study in Scotland. You will be entitled to take out a **Tuition Fee Loan** to cover these costs in full (page 16). The good news is that the set tuition fee in Scotland is generally lower than the variable fees charged in England: £1,820 per year for new students entering a first degree course (£2,895 for Medicine). However, you need to take into account that you will be unlikely to receive a bursary from a Scottish university.

### How to apply

For your main student finance package – Tuition Fee Loan, Maintenance Loan and Maintenance Grant – contact the student finance provider for your country (page 13).

**FOUR-YEAR DEGREES**
Standard degree courses in Scotland are four years long, but students from the rest of the UK still pay less overall in tuition fees than if they studied in their home country.

## ● EU students from other countries

This section applies to you if you are an EU national (but not from the UK) and are studying, or plan to study, full-time in the UK. It is also relevant to nationals from EU overseas territories and Switzerland, Iceland, Norway and Liechtenstein. See page 76 for information on studying part-time in the UK.

## a) EU students studying in England, Northern Ireland or Wales

If you are applying for a full-time undergraduate degree course at a university in England, Northern Ireland or Wales you will be eligible for a **Tuition Fee Loan** on the same basis as English students (page 16), though not a Maintenance Loan. The Tuition Fee Loan is not means-tested and the maximum you can borrow depends on the fees charged by your university. To apply, download an application form from www.direct.gov.uk/ studentfinance-EU, complete the form and return it to the Student Finance Services European Team (the address is on the website) by the relevant deadline. Or if you are applying through UCAS, they will send you an application form for the loan when you are offered a place on a course.

You may also qualify for a **Tuition Fee Grant** if you are studying in Wales. This is £1,940 for 2009/10 irrespective of household income (page 59).

See the section on extra help through **bursaries**, **scholarships** and **awards** (pages 29–51) as you may be eligible to apply for a bursary or scholarship at your chosen university. There may also be awards available from trusts and charities on top of the student finance package provided by the government (page 49).

If you have lived in the UK for three years or more by the time you start your course then you will be entitled to the same level of support as students who normally live in England, Northern Ireland or Wales. In other words, you can apply for help to cover living costs as well as tuition fees (i.e. a **Maintenance Loan** – see page 17). To apply, follow the same procedure as UK students and, to check if you qualify, contact the Student Finance Services European Team (as above).

## b) EU students studying in Scotland

As a EU national applying to study for a first degree in Scotland, your student finance application should be through the Student Awards Agency for Scotland (SAAS) – www.saas.gov.uk. If your main reason for coming to Scotland is to study full-time, the SAAS will pay your tuition fees but you won't get any maintenance support. You need to apply for each year of your study to have your tuition fee paid, in the same way as Scottish students studying in Scotland (page 63).

If you are already resident in the UK, or if you meet certain conditions regarding migrant workers or self-employed persons (check the SAAS website for details), you may also be entitled to help with your living costs – in effect the full-support package available to Scottish students studying in Scotland: a **Maintenance Loan**, **Young Students' Bursary**, an **Additional Loan**, **Travel Expenses Grant** and any relevant **Supplementary Grants** (pages 63–6).

➡ **EU STUDENT NUMBERS ARE RISING**
Between 2006/07 and 2007/08 the number of EU students from outside the UK choosing to study at UK higher education institutions rose by 6 per cent (from 105,410 to 112,150).

## ● International students (non-EU)

If you do not have either 'home' or EU student status you will not have access to UK government support for fees or living costs. The fees for international students are unregulated and usually much higher than fees charged to UK students (pages 129–30), making it difficult for many overseas students without considerable funds of their own to come to the UK to study. However, there are scholarships and awards available, even if they don't cover the whole cost of studying here. Try contacting your country's ministry of education as they may have scholarship opportunities for students wishing to study overseas. There are also scholarships available for international students through the British Council and other charitable organisations, but competition is strong, and many are only for postgraduate courses. Check the British Council website (www.britishcouncil. org), which provides an online database giving information on approximately 270 individual awards from UK educational establishments, charities and professional bodies, and a free booklet to download with information about how to apply for a grant or scholarship. You'll also find contact details for a British Council office in your own country.

There is useful information on visas, overseas fees, funding and working in the UK while you are studying at www.ukcisa.org.uk (UK Council for International Student Affairs). See also www.ukstudentlife.com. For information on paying tax in the UK when you are working, see page 122.

It is possible to become a 'home' fee payer and have eligibility for funding from the UK, for example, if you are a refugee or someone with Humanitarian Protection or Discretionary Leave – for further details see www.ukcisa.org.uk.

**➤ INTERNATIONAL STUDENT NUMBERS ARE RISING**
UK qualifications are internationally recognised and highly valued. Each year many thousands of international students come to the UK to study for a degree, and the numbers have been on the increase: from 220,375 to 229,640 between 2006/07 and 2007/08 (a rise of 4 per cent).

*The Bob the Builder theme tune was composed by a Biology graduate from Trent Polytechnic (now Nottingham Trent University), Paul Joyce.*

# 9 Special cases

This chapter covers the funding arrangements for independent students, students with children or adult dependants, students with disabilities, and part-time students. There is also information on financial support for specialist courses such as Medicine, sandwich courses incorporating an industrial placement, language or other courses with time spent abroad, and Foundation year courses.

## ● Independent students

As far as student finance is concerned, it is whether you are classified as an independent student or not that is important. You are treated as an independent student if you are aged 25 or over. However, even some students under the age of 21 are considered to be independent if they are married or in a civil partnership; have no living parents; are permanently estranged from their parents; have supported themselves for three years; or have dependent children of their own.

If you are deemed independent then your parents' income will not be taken into account for the purposes of means-testing your Student Loan and Grant. Instead your own income will be assessed, together with the income of your spouse or civil partner. If you have a cohabiting partner of either sex and you are over 25, then your partner's income will be included in the assessment.

## SPONSORSHIP TIP

If you are currently working but plan to go to university to study, try approaching your employer for financial support during your studies. Your employer may be interested in sponsoring you if you intend to continue working with them after the course has ended. See pages 102–4 on sponsorship.

## Age limits for student finance

To qualify for a **Maintenance Loan** you need to be aged under 60 when you start your course (50 in Scotland). There are no upper age limits for grants or the **Tuition Fee Loan**.

## Previous study

Tuition Fee Loans are generally available for the full length of your course, plus one extra year if needed. If you have previously studied at a higher education institution, this period may be affected. For example, if you already have a

### Student Talk

'I am a mature student. I obtained a full loan plus a small grant – but have lost a substantial income in return. I am hoping to find paid work this summer and to get away with under £15,000 of debt for the whole three years. I love being a student – my main advice is don't stress – just enjoy!'

degree then you cannot have a Maintenance Loan – although there are certain courses exempt from this policy, such as those leading to professional qualifications (Medicine, Dentistry, Veterinary Science, Nursing, Teaching, etc). You may be eligible for **Supplementary Grants** even if you have previously studied in the UK.

● **Students with children or adult dependants**

Students with dependants can be considered for three means-tested **Supplementary Grants**: the Childcare Grant, the Parents' Learning Allowance and the Adult Dependants' Grant. None of these grants has to be repaid and all are means-tested. Note that there are different arrangements in Scotland for students with children and adult dependants, including a Lone Parent's Grant. See www.saas.gov.uk for more information.

The **Childcare Grant** is for full-time students with children aged under 15 to help with childcare costs. It can cover 85 per cent of your actual childcare costs during term times and holidays, depending on your household income. The maximum available in England and Northern Ireland for one child is £148.75 a week (£161.50 a week in Wales) and £255 a week if you have two or more children (£274.55 a week in Wales). There is no Childcare Grant in Scotland but students with children can receive help through the tax credits system.

You may also be eligible for the **Parents' Learning Allowance**, which gives help towards course-related costs for students with dependent children. The amount in England and Northern Ireland is between £50 and £1,508 a year (£50 and

£1,508 in Wales) and depends on your household income. You can apply for a Parents' Learning Allowance whether or not you get the Childcare Grant. The PLA is being discontinued for English domiciled students from 2010/11. Child tax credits are also available for students with children.

If you are studying full-time and have a partner or another adult who depends on you financially you may be eligible for an **Adult Dependants' Grant** of up to £2,642 a year in England and Northern Ireland (£2,647 in Wales and £2,640 in Scotland), depending on your household income.

### Applying for Supplementary Grants

Complete the relevant sections on your main student finance application (the one you use to apply for a Student Loan and Grant).

### ● Disabled students

Students with a disability or a specific learning difficulty like dyslexia can receive extra support through the **Disabled Students' Allowance,** which is intended to help disabled people to study on an equal basis with other students. The allowance is not means-tested so your household income has no effect on the amount you receive; it is based on an assessment of your individual needs, up to a maximum amount (see below). It does not have to be repaid and is available on top of the standard student finance package. Both full-time and part-time students on courses lasting at least one year can apply, including students on distance-learning courses. For more information on eligibility, go to www.direct.gov.uk/studentfinance (or your own country's student finance provider if you are not from England – page 13).

## DISABLED STUDENTS' ALLOWANCE IN ENGLAND 2009/10

| Disabled Students' Allowance | Full-time students (max. available) | Part-time students (max. available) |
|---|---|---|
| Non-medical helper, e.g. a note-taker | £20,520 a year | £15,390 a year |
| Major items of specialist equipment you need for studying, e.g. computer software | £5,161 for the whole course | £5,161 for the whole course |
| General Disabled Students' Allowances | £1,724 a year | £1,293 a year |

The maximum figures for the Disabled Students' Allowance in the other countries are similar.

There is useful information for students with disabilities at www.skill.org.uk.

● **Part-time and distance learning students**

Government funding for undergraduates studying on a part-time basis, or by distance learning, generally differs from the standard student finance package offered to full-time students. How much you will get depends on where you plan to study and which course: some courses attract special, more generous part-time funding arrangements than others, for example, Health Professional courses (pages 89–94), Social Work courses (page 94) and Initial Teacher Training courses (page 96).

**→ PART-TIME DEGREES**
**Eleven per cent of first degree graduates gained their award through part-time study in 2007/08 (that's 37,655 students out of a total of 334,890). (Source: HESA – Higher Education Statistics Agency)**

## a) Studying part-time in England

Part-time students studying in England can apply for:

• **a Fee Grant** (to help with tuition fees) – paid directly to your college or university.

• **a Course Grant** (to help with study costs, such as books, materials and travel) – paid directly into your bank account in one lump sum.

You don't need to pay back the money awarded in a Fee Grant or a Course Grant. The amount you will receive depends on your household income, how 'intensive' your course is (how long it will take to complete compared to an equivalent full-time course) and how much the fees are. For the most intensive courses (equivalent to 75 per cent of a full-time course), a maximum of £1,470 is available through the Fee Grant and Course Grant combined in 2009/10. The maximum Fee Grant is £1,210, but if your fees are less than this then the most you can get will be the cost of your fees. If your fees are more, you will need to make up the difference.

To check your eligibility and to download an application form, go to www.direct.gov.uk/studentfinance (the section for part-time students), or telephone 0800 731 9133 for a paper copy. You'll need to apply for each academic year.

Some universities run an **Additional Fee Support Scheme**. This can help cover any part of your fees that isn't covered by the Fee Grant if you are on a low income and can't continue your course without extra support. The **Access to Learning Fund** may also provide funds if you get into financial difficulties (page 52). If you have children or adult dependants, you may be eligible for a partial payment of a **Supplementary Grant** such as the **Adult Dependants' Grant**, **Childcare Grant** and **Parents' Learning Allowance**, depending on the intensity of your course and whether it qualifies – check with your university. Part-time students on a course that lasts at least one year may be eligible for a **Disabled Students' Allowance** (page 75).

Other funding options include **educational trusts and charities** (page 49) and **Career Development Loans** (page 98).

### FEE GRANT AND COURSE GRANT (ENGLAND), 2009/10

| Intensity of course | Fee grant (max.) | Course grant (max.) | Total support (max.) |
|---|---|---|---|
| Equivalent to 50–59% of full-time course | £805 | £260 | £1,065 |
| Equivalent to 60–74% of full-time course | £970 | £260 | £1,230 |
| Equivalent to 75% or more of full-time course | £1,210 | £260 | £1,470 |

### b) Studying part-time in Northern Ireland

The **Fee Grant** and **Course Grant** are the same as for England. For more information go to www.studentfinanceni.co.uk (part-time students).

## c) Studying part-time in Wales

The maximum **Fee Grant** in Wales is lower than in England but the **Course Grant** is much higher. How much you get will be calculated by your Local Authority and will depend on the intensity of your course as well as your household income. These are the maximum figures:

**FEE GRANT AND COURSE GRANT (WALES), 2009/10**

| Intensity of course | Fee grant (max.) | Course grant (max.) |
|---|---|---|
| 50–59% | £635 | £1,075 |
| 60%–74% | £765 | £1,075 |
| 75% or more | £955 | £1,075 |

## d) Studying part-time in Scotland

A **Part-time Grant** of up to £500 to help towards the cost of your tuition fees is available to all new and existing students aged 16 or over, earning £22,000 or less and who are studying at a rate of 50 per cent or more of a full-time course. The grant does not need to be repaid. For more information, see the SAAS website at www.saas.gov.uk or contact the ILA Scotland helpline 0808 100 1090 (www.ilascotland.org.uk).

## e) Distance learning with the Open University

You can apply to the Open University for a **Fee Grant** and a **Course Grant** to study for a degree by distance learning if your household income is below a certain level. If applicable, you can also apply for a **Disabled Students' Allowance** (page 75). For more information, check the Open University website: www.open.ac.uk.

➡ **OPEN UNIVERSITY FACTS**

• The number of young people choosing the Open University (OU) over a conventional university has increased dramatically over the last decade. The Open University is now the largest university in the UK, with 176,560 students. The next largest is the University of Manchester with 39,165 students. The smallest is the University of Buckingham with 840 students. (Source: Universities UK, 2008)

• The typical cost of an OU degree is £3,500–£4,000 for five or six years' study, depending on the course. This looks good value when you compare the cost of attending a three-year degree course at a conventional university, which can add up to £30,000 or more when you factor in yearly costs of tuition and accommodation, etc.

## f) EU students studying part-time in the UK

As a part-time or distance-learning EU student, who is not from the UK but is living in the UK and earning a low income, you may be eligible for the same funding as 'home' students (UK nationals). See page 76 for more details, and as follows:

• For England, Wales and Northern Ireland: www.direct. gov.uk/studentfinance (the section for part-time students).

• For Scotland: ILA Scotland helpline 0808 100 1090 (www.ilascotland.org.uk).

## ● Sandwich courses with industrial placements

A well-paid industrial placement will help to clear some of your student debts and can provide valuable experience that may further your career. 'Sandwich' degrees incorporating a paid industrial placement include engineering, business studies, marketing, finance and computer science. Special funding arrangements apply for these courses.

During your year on placement you will have to pay the tuition fee for your course, although at a reduced rate if you are away from the university for a full year. The university will set the reduced amount, up to 50 per cent off the current fee. For a shorter placement of less than a year, full fees will be charged (up to £3,225 for 2009/10). A **Tuition Fee Loan** and **Maintenance Loan** are still available for your placement year, but the Maintenance Loan will be at a reduced rate (around 50 per cent of the standard loan). The same applies if you are on an unpaid full-year placement, unless it is in the voluntary or public sectors, such as in a hospital, in which case you are eligible for the full Maintenance Loan, which is means-tested (page 15). Bursaries are not normally paid during a year on placement. On part-year placements (paid or unpaid) you are eligible for the normal rates of Maintenance Loan.

As a Scottish student on a compulsory paid placement, you will not have to pay fees during your course or your placement, but you'll need to apply to the SAAS each year to have your fees paid for you. During the placement you will be eligible for the full means-tested Maintenance Loan but the Young Students' Bursary, Students Outside Scotland Bursary and Additional Loan will not be available.

## Finding a placement

• Check with your course organisers as they may well have lists of companies offering work experience.

• The Year in Industry (YINI) programme provides paid placements with companies across the UK for science, engineering and technology students in their gap year or during their degree course. Placements normally begin in the summer or autumn so apply in the autumn before you wish to start

**FIRST 'SANDWICH' COURSES**
The University of Sunderland was the first university in England to introduce the 'sandwich' course, enabling engineering apprentices to gain higher qualifications while working. By 1908, 25 local engineering firms were involved in the scheme.

your placement. There's an application form to download from the website www.yini.org.uk. Once your application has been processed you will be interviewed and your details circulated to selected partner companies, who will then shortlist for further interviews. There is a £25 fee to enter the scheme, which doesn't guarantee you a placement but you can introduce a friend and have your registration fee refunded. You can also opt for a year's work experience combined with an overseas travel experience in the summer. For more information, visit the YINI website.

• See also the placements abroad organised by IAESTE – page 85.

**Student Talk**

'I did an industrial placement as part of my first degree. I was employed at a company, so was paid a wage and that was how I funded the year.'

## ● Studying and working abroad: language and other courses

UK students are being encouraged through various incentives to study or work abroad for part of their degree. Some students choose to study for their whole degree in a country outside the UK.

There are many advantages to studying and working abroad, such as:

- Learning another language – research shows that applicants with language abilities are viewed more favourably in the job market than those without such skills. (Source: Council for Industry and Higher Education)
- Gaining skills, experience and an international perspective that will look good on your CV.
- Building up an international network of friends and work associates.
- Making financial savings due to lower fees (especially universities elsewhere in Europe) or a lower cost of living.
- Taking advantage of scholarship schemes available for international students (e.g. in the USA).
- Having a good deal of fun – many students who have studied or worked abroad say it was one of the best parts of their university life.

### a) Studying and working abroad as part of your UK degree

Language courses usually offer the opportunity to study or work in another country as part of your UK degree, but remember that studying abroad isn't just for language students. Exchange schemes such as Erasmus (see below) are open to students from a wide range of degree courses. Some European universities offer several courses in English, so you may not even have to speak a foreign language. There are also summer schools for students from all disciplines who want to work abroad during the vacations.

Your studies in another EU country should receive full academic recognition from your home university under the European Credit Transfer Accumulation System (ECTS). Check with the International Office or Study Abroad Office at your university about opportunities available for your particular course.

If you study or work abroad as part of your UK degree you may be eligible for:
- an overseas rate of **Maintenance Loan** if you study abroad for at least one term – the maximum rate for English students is £5,895 (check with your student finance provider if you are not from England – page 13).
- a **Travel Grant** to help with travel costs related to your placement or study abroad, which is subject to a means test and equal to the amount you reasonably have to pay, minus the first £303. You may also be able to get help to cover the costs of medical insurance, visas and vaccinations.
- a **Tuition Fee Loan** to cover the cost of the tuition fee you will have to pay to your home university for the year you are away. The fee may be reduced if you are away for a year (for example, by 50 per cent), but for a placement of less than a full year, a full fee will be charged.
- an **Erasmus Scheme Grant** if you study or work abroad for a period of between three months and one academic year in any of the 31 European countries participating in the scheme. The grant, which is not means-tested and doesn't need to be repaid, is a contribution towards the extra costs

arising from studying abroad. It is not intended to cover all of your essential living costs (for 2008/09 the average grant for studying abroad was around €245 per month). As part of the scheme, you do not have to pay a tuition fee at the university you are visiting, and if you spend a full year abroad on an Erasmus placement you should also be exempt from paying the reduced fee that sandwich students taking a year out normally have to pay. You can still receive any Student Loans or Grants to which you are entitled (see above). Students from all disciplines can participate, not just language students, but check with your home institution as not all institutions offer Erasmus for all subjects. For more details on the Erasmus programme (which is run by the European Union's Lifelong Learning Programme) visit the website www.erasmus.ac.uk.

• a **salary** on a placement. For example, the IAESTE (International Association for the Exchange of Students for Technical Experience) scheme administered by the British Council organises technical work experience abroad for science, engineering, technology and architecture undergraduates. The placements, which provide course-related work in industry, research institutions and the public sector, usually take place in the summer months for 8 to 12 weeks. You will earn a salary to cover the local cost of living and receive assistance with work permits, visas and accommodation. In many cases there are organised social activities. For more information, see www.iaeste.org.uk.

For general help and advice on all aspects of studying abroad, check out the pages for UK students studying abroad on the UK Council for International Student Affairs (UKCISA) website (www.ukcisa.org.uk).

**Student Talk**

*'I'm about to go on a compulsory year abroad. I've applied through the British Council to be a language assistant in a French school. There is so much funding available: at my university, fees are waived for the year, but you still get Maintenance Grants and Loans from the Student Loans Company. In addition, you get an Erasmus Grant (€200–300 a month), and language assistants also get paid for their work. They don't call it a pay-off-your-overdraft-year for nothing!'*

## b) Doing a whole degree course abroad

While UK universities have a worldwide reputation, the UK is not the only country with good universities. You may dream of doing your first degree in the USA or a Commonwealth country and every year such dreams become a reality for some students. For example, about 8,400 UK undergraduates are enrolled at US universities. Many more go overseas for further study or employment once they have graduated.

The most common destinations are other English-speaking countries, including Australia, Canada, Ireland and the USA, and plenty of advice and information is available. For example, there is a regular 'College Day' in London organised by the

Fulbright Commission, when around 100 US universities come to extol the virtues of an American university education. Interest for possible study in other countries has grown since the introduction of higher fees in the UK from 2006. There are also university ranking tables for each of the major English-speaking countries – check the links at www.thecompleteuni versityguide.co.uk (under Students – Choosing a University – Overseas university).

You need to plan well ahead if you want to study at a university based overseas – probably 12 to 18 months in advance of the start of the course.

As you will be studying for the whole of your degree at a non-UK institution you will not be eligible for UK student

### ➡ STUDY ABROAD COSTS

Costs can add up when you study for a whole degree abroad, especially if the value of the pound is low in relation to the currency of the country you are visiting. You may not need to pay high tuition fees at an EU university, but you won't get a Student Loan or Grant from the UK so you'll have to find other ways to cover your costs of going to university. In France, for example, your course fee could be around €150–500 per annum in a public institution, accommodation might add up to €300 a month, food and socialising could cost around €300 a month, and travel might average €450–600 a year. Then there are additional costs, such as insurance (health and possessions), university registration fees, study materials, Internet, clothes, etc. You'll have to think realistically about whether you will get a part-time job to finance your way. In the US, tuition fees can be very high. For example, at Yale the annual tuition fee is more than $30,000, though there are initiatives that extend to the UK aimed at making Yale and similar places affordable for students from low-income households. Contact the universities direct for relevant information.

funding. Generally there are only low tuition fees to pay for courses in non-UK European public institutions so the main costs you will need to cover are accommodation, meals and transport, all of which will vary according to the country you choose. If you choose to study outside the EU, your costs are likely to be higher as you will normally pay international student fees. The high cost of travelling beyond the EU might also be a factor. Occasionally, there are scholarships available for overseas students, although these are often reserved for postgraduates – check with the university to which you are applying.

For more information about visas and other formalities, go to www.ukcisa.org.uk (UK Council for International Student Affairs) – under 'advice for UK students studying abroad'.

## ● Foundation year courses

Some courses incorporate a Foundation year designed as a first step to a degree course, often aimed at students who lack the typical entry qualifications. These courses provide a platform on which to progress in your chosen area of study. Funding for a Foundation year is the same as for other courses (see chapters 3–8) if certain conditions are met:

• The Foundation course must be a first step to a degree course and not a stand-alone course designed to lead directly to employment.

• You register for the full degree, not just the Foundation course.

• The degree course must be eligible for student funding – check with the university and your student finance provider.

• If you achieve a high grade from your Foundation year you may be eligible for a scholarship from your university.

## ● Medicine and Dentistry courses

For those of you on a standard five- or six-year medical or dental course, the first four years of your finance package will be the same as for most other students. You can apply for a **Tuition Fee Loan**, **Maintenance Loan** and **Maintenance Grant** to pay your tuition fee and contribute towards your living costs.

For the fifth and subsequent years, you can apply for a means-tested **NHS Bursary**. The basic rates of the bursary in 2009/10 are £2,346 a year (living in your parents' home), £3,392 a year (living in London) and £2,810 a year (living elsewhere). There is extra available for longer courses (over 30 weeks). The amount you get may be reduced depending on the household income of your parents or your spouse or civil partner. Your tuition fees for the fifth and subsequent years are paid in full by the NHS as part of this scheme. The scheme is administered by the NHS Business Services Authority (NHSBSA) and you can check how much you are likely to receive using their online bursary calculator at www.nhsbsa.nhs.uk. All UK students on qualifying courses are eligible, and non-UK students from the EU may also be eligible if they satisfy certain residency conditions (such as living for the majority of the time in the UK for three years prior to the start of the academic year). NHS Bursaries are paid in monthly instalments.

The NHS Bursary is not intended to cover all your living costs, so to make up the difference you can apply for a reduced rate (approximately 50 per cent) **Maintenance Loan** from the Student Loans Company (page 17). This loan – unlike the Maintenance Loans for non-healthcare students – is not means-tested. **Hardship Funds** (for example, **Access for Learning** in

**➡ WORKING IN THE NHS**
You are not obliged to work in the NHS when you qualify if
you've received an NHS bursary to help finance your studies, but you
will be encouraged to develop at least some of your career in the NHS
or in the Social Care services.

England) may be available to you if you are in financial difficulty (page 52), and means-tested **Supplementary Grants** if you
have children, adult dependants (page 74) and/or if you have
disabilities (pages 75–6).

Medical and dental students can receive a means-tested grant
for **Practice Placement Expenses** such as travel costs related to
placements (including travel abroad if you have to attend an estab-
lishment outside the UK as part of your course). In addition, you
may be eligible for help to cover the cost of medical insurance if
you have to study abroad for at least 50 per cent of the term.

## How to apply

Apply for an **NHS Bursary** when you have been offered an
NHS-funded place (either conditionally or unconditionally) at
university. Your university will advise NHSBSA when you have
been accepted and you will then be sent a bursary application
form by NHS Student Bursaries.

## Studying part-time?

You are still eligible for an **NHS Bursary**, normally at 75 per
cent of the full-time rate. Any **Disability Allowances** will be
paid in full, and **Practice Placement Expenses** are also paid.

## Arrangements in different countries of the UK

Broadly comparable arrangements are available for Scottish,
Welsh and Northern Irish students (in Scotland it is the

'Scottish Government Health Directorate Bursary' and the basic rates of income-assessed bursary are slightly lower than the figures above; in Northern Ireland it is the DHSSPS Bursary). For more details contact the university of your choice and the relevant authorities which assess and pay the bursaries:

• England: NHSBSA Student Bursaries, www.nhsbsa. nhs.uk
• Northern Ireland: apply to your local Education and Library Board – www.delni.gov.uk/further-and-higher-educa- tion/studfin-useful-addresses (North Eastern Education and Library Board for English, Welsh and Scottish students studying in NI).
• Wales: The NHS Wales Student Award Unit, www.nliah. wales.nhs.uk
• Scotland: The Students Awards Agency for Scotland, www.saas.gov.uk

There is a separate **Dental Bursary** scheme (currently £4,000/year) in Scotland for all students from year two onwards studying for a Dentistry degree at Dundee and Glasgow, and for the full four years for students at Aberdeen. Students who receive the bursary have to sign up for five years (or part-time equivalent) of NHS dentistry work in Scotland after gradua- tion. For more information, check the SAAS website (www.saas.gov.uk), or telephone 0131 244 4519.

## ● Allied Health Professional courses

If you are taking a course (part-time or full-time) leading to professional registration in one of the Allied Health Professions, you are also eligible for a means-tested **NHS**

**Bursary**. Unlike Medicine and Dentistry students, you'll receive the bursary from year one. The UK health authorities will pay your tuition fees in full.

The relevant courses are: Audiology, Chiropody or Podiatry, Dental Hygiene or Dental Therapy, Dietetics, Occupational Therapy, Orthoptics, Physiotherapy, Prosthetics and Orthotics, Radiography, and Speech and Language Therapy.

You may also be entitled to a reduced rate (approximately 50 per cent) **Maintenance Loan** (page 17) on top of the NHS Bursary (the loan is not means-tested), **Supplementary Grants** (page 74) and reimbursement for **Practice Placement Expenses** (page 90).

Broadly comparable arrangements are available for Scottish, Welsh and Northern Irish students (in Scotland, the bursary is known as the 'Scottish Government Health Directorate Bursary'). For more details, contact the relevant national authorities which assess and pay the bursaries (page 91).

### ● Nursing and Midwifery courses

Students with NHS-funded places on degree courses leading to registration as a nurse or a midwife have their tuition fees paid in full by the NHS and may be eligible for a means-tested **NHS Bursary**. The NHS Student Bursary Calculator at www.nhsbsa.nhs.uk will give you an estimate of what you might get, or telephone NHSBSA Student Bursaries for more information (0845 358 6655). On top of the NHS Bursary, you may be entitled to a reduced rate (approximately 50 per cent) **Maintenance Loan** from the Student Loans Company (page 17), which – like the loans for other healthcare students – is not means-tested. If you are in financial difficulty, you may be eligible for **Hardship Funds** (page 52), and means-tested **Supplementary Grants** if you have children or adult dependants (page 74) and/or if you have disabilities (page 75). An **Initial Expenses Allowance** of around £55 at the start of the course and **Practice Placement Expenses** (page 90) to cover travel costs to training placements in hospitals or community health services may also be available. If you choose a diploma of higher education pre-registration nursing course instead of a degree course, you may be eligible for a higher, non means-tested NHS Bursary, but you won't be eligible for a Maintenance Loan.

## How to apply

Apply for an NHS Bursary when you have been offered an NHS-funded place (either conditionally or unconditionally) at university. Your university will advise NHSBSA when you have been successful and you will then be sent a bursary application form by NHS Student Bursaries.

## Studying part-time?

Nursing degree students studying part-time are eligible for the means-tested NHS Bursary at an appropriate proportion of the full-time rate. Any **Supplementary Grants** for disabilities will be paid in full and **Practice Placement Expenses** are also given.

## Arrangements in different countries of the UK

Broadly comparable arrangements are available for Scottish and Welsh students. In Scotland, the Scottish Government Health Directorate (SGHD) pays the tuition fees and a non means-tested bursary under the Nursing and Midwifery Bursary Scheme (NMSB). Under a special arrangement with the Department of

Health, English, Welsh and Northern Irish students taking courses in Nursing and Midwifery at Scottish institutions may be given
support from the NMSB scheme. For more details, contact the
relevant authorities which assess and pay the bursaries (page 91).
The Central Services Agency deals with bursaries for students
from Northern Ireland studying on a pre-registration Nursing
and Midwifery course there.

### Social Work courses

Introduced as an incentive for people to train in social
work, the **Social Work Bursary** is not means-tested and is
available to English, Welsh and Northern Irish students on eligible courses in the UK who don't already get funding from
their employer (there are no Social Work Bursaries for Scottish
students). The Social Work Bursary doesn't need to be repaid
and can be used towards study-related expenses, for travel costs
incurred while carrying out your placement duties, or in any
manner that best suits your individual circumstances. You can
check if your course in England is eligible (i.e. approved by the
General Social Care Council) at www.gscc.org.uk under the section 'Becoming a social worker'. If you are taking a course in
Wales or Northern Ireland, see the table opposite for checking
course eligibility.

The amount of the bursary is dependent on where you study,
whether you are studying full-time or part-time, and whether
your course attracts tuition fees. As a guide, if you are studying
full-time at a university outside London, on an undergraduate
course subject to tuition fees, you might be eligible for a bursary
of £4,575 for a 52-week period and you would be responsible for
paying your tuition fee. You would have the option to use some

of your bursary to pay your fee or apply for a **Tuition Fee Loan**
from the Student Loans Company along with the standard student finance package (pages 15–28) – but you don't need to
qualify for the standard package to get the Social Work Bursary.

Note that you must apply each year for the Social Work
Bursary and the bursary may affect your entitlement to other
benefits and allowances.

## FUNDING AUTHORITIES FOR SOCIAL WORK UNDERGRADUATES

| Where you normally live | Where you are studying | Funding authority for Social Work courses | List of approved Social Work courses |
| --- | --- | --- | --- |
| England | England, Northern Ireland, Scotland or Wales | NHS Business Services Authority (NHSBSA) www.nhsbsa.nhs.uk | www.gscc.org.uk |
| Scotland | England, Northern Ireland, Scotland or Wales | Bursaries are not available to undergraduates | Not applicable |
| Wales | England, Northern Ireland, Scotland or Wales | Care Council for Wales www.ccwales.org.uk | www.ccwales.org.uk |
| Northern Ireland | Northern Ireland | Social Services Inspectorate (Northern Ireland), Social Work Student Incentive Scheme www.dhsspsni.gov.uk | www.niscc.info |

**How to apply**

In England the bursary is administered by the NHS Business Services Authority (Prescription Pricing Division) and the application form can be found on their website (www. nhsbsa.nhs.uk). In Northern Ireland and Wales you must have been accepted on an approved Social Work degree course. Your chosen university will send you an application form. There are no Social Work bursaries available in Scotland. The Social Services Inspectorate (SSI) at the Department of Health, Social Services and Public Safety (DHSSPS) provides a bursary scheme for Northern Irish students studying approved degree courses in social work in Northern Ireland.

● **Initial Teacher Training courses**

Training to be a teacher? Then special funding arrangements for Initial Teacher Training (ITT) courses apply in England – see opposite.

Students from Northern Ireland, Scotland and Wales should contact their student finance providers for information on the full range of student support available for training teachers (page 13).

## ITT FUNDING ARRANGEMENTS IN ENGLAND

| ITT course | Funding available |
|---|---|
| Full-time undergraduate | Eligible for the same finance package as other full-time students, i.e. Tuition Fee Loan, Maintenance Loan, Maintenance Grant or Special Support Grant, etc (pages 15–28). You may also qualify for a bursary from your university (page 29) and Supplementary Grants if you have a dependant child or adult or a disability (pages 74–6). |
| Part-time (where the course doesn't take more than twice as long as an equivalent full-time course) | Eligible for elements of the student finance package (even though it's usually only available to full-time undergraduate students), for example, a Tuition Fee Loan, Maintenance Loan and Maintenance Grant or Special Support Grant. The maximum loan depends on your household income, how many weeks of the year you spend on full-time study and teaching practice, and where you study. If you spend 6–10 weeks on full-time study and teaching practice, you can get a Maintenance Loan of up to £4,950 if you live away from home (and more if you study in London). If you spend fewer than six weeks, your Maintenance Loan will be around half this. You may also qualify for Supplementary Grants such as the Childcare Grant, Parents' Learning Allowance and/or the Adult Dependants' Grant (pages 74–6) if you spend at least six weeks a year on full-time study and teaching practice. |

*The University of Bedfordshire*
*currently owns two islands in cyberspace*
*in 'Second Life': the University of*
*Bedfordshire island and Bedfordia.*

# 10    Career Development Loans

Don't panic if you are not eligible for any of the financial support already mentioned as there are other ways to raise funds to go to university. One option is to apply for a **Career Development Loan** (CDL), available through high street banks in partnership with the government's Learning and Skills Council (LSC). CDLs are intended to remove financial barriers to learning and to get more people from a wide range of educational and employment backgrounds to take responsibility for their own vocational (work-related) studies and training. Like the Student Loan, a CDL has to be paid back, but there are important differences, as you can see in the table opposite.

## ● Who qualifies for a CDL and which courses apply?

You can apply for a CDL if you normally live in England, Scotland or Wales and intend to work in the EU (or Iceland, Norway or Liechtenstein) when you have finished your course. You can't have a CDL if you are entitled to some other type of publicly-funded support, such as a Student Loan or Grant.

To qualify for a CDL, you must show that the course you want to follow will improve your job skills. It can be full-time,

## COMPARING STUDENT LOANS AND CAREER DEVELOPMENT LOANS

| Student Loan | Career Development Loan (CDL) |
| --- | --- |
| You don't start repaying a Student Loan until you are earning over £15,000 per annum. | You begin repaying your CDL one month after your course ends regardless of your income at the time. You can postpone repayments up to 17 months under certain circumstances but you must agree this with the bank before repayments are due to start. |
| Repayments are always linked to your salary so you stop making repayments during any period when your salary is below £15,000. The repayments end when your loan is paid off, or after 25 years, whichever is sooner. | Repayments are not linked to your salary. You can repay the loan over a period of between 12 months and 5 years. The repayments remain fixed once your loan has been agreed. |
| The interest you pay covers only the rise in inflation during the term of your loan, so in effect what you borrow is the same as the amount you repay. | A CDL is interest-free up to one month after the end of your course (the government pays the interest up to this point). After this you pay a commercial rate of interest so what you pay back over the full term of the loan is more than what you borrow. A typical example: you borrow £4,500 for a 12-month course. - repayable by 24 monthly payments of £212.22 - total amount payable: £5,093.28 (12.9% APR) |

For both types of loan, if you fail to complete your course you are still responsible for paying back the full loan amount. You must speak with your bank/student finance provider without delay if your circumstances change.

part-time, or distance learning; undergraduate or postgraduate. The course provider must be on the CDL Register of
Learning Providers, which is organised by the Learning and
Skills Council in England (telephone 0870 900 6800,
www.lsc.gov.uk). Some courses are not eligible; for example,
Foundation year courses used as a first step to a degree course
(page 88), although stand-alone Foundation courses that lead
to employment would be eligible. See www.direct. gov.uk/cdl
for more details.

A CDL can help to pay for up to two years of learning or up
to three years if the course includes one year's relevant practical
work experience. If your course lasts longer than this, you may
still be able to use a CDL to pay for part of it.

### ● How much can you get?

Between £300 and £8,000, paid in stages or in one lump
sum, to help towards the cost of fees, course costs (books,
childcare, travel expenses, costs associated with a disability, etc)
and living expenses. You will need to calculate your monthly living expenses and the bank will help you to work out a realistic
repayment rate and schedule. If you are on benefits, receiving a
CDL may affect your benefits entitlement so check with your
Benefit Office before applying for a CDL.

### ● How do you repay the loan?

You repay the loan to the bank over an agreed period at a
fixed rate of interest.

## Choosing a bank

CDLs are provided by three high street banks:

- Barclays (www.barclays.co.uk)
- The Co-operative Bank (www.co-operativebank.co.uk)
- The Royal Bank of Scotland (www.rbs.co.uk)

Interest rates may vary from bank to bank.

**REPAYMENT TIP**

Make sure you know what the repayments will be after you've finished your course and that you are confident you can meet them.

## How to apply

Call the CDL helpline on 0800 585 505 to ask for an application pack and for advice. You can also book a free call with a CDL advisor by emailing them first – use the relevant link at www.direct.gov.uk/cdl.

Apply well in advance of your course so you have plenty of time to apply to another bank if you don't succeed first time round. You can't apply to more than one bank at a time. In exceptional circumstances you can apply after you have started your course, but there needs to be enough time to process your application before the course ends. You may have to wait four weeks for an answer from the bank and the bank cannot release any funds until your university has confirmed your place. The bank will pay any course fees directly to your course provider and money for living expenses directly into your bank account.

**LOAN APPROVAL TIP**

The banks have the right to refuse an application for a Career Development Loan, even if you are eligible on paper and have been offered a place at university. So it's best not to start a course until you have approval of the loan.

## 11  Sponsorship by employers

One of the best ways to finance your way through university is to be sponsored by an employer. Sponsorship gives you money during term time and a job during the vacations. But competition is fierce and you need to be determined and well organised to find a suitable sponsor.

### ● Benefits of sponsorship

- A sense of achievement: sponsorship is highly regarded.
- Less financial pressure at university.
- Money from your sponsor during term time and useful work experience with your sponsor during vacations.
- New skills.
- The possibility of a full-time job with your sponsor when you graduate (though there are no guarantees).
- Helpful material for your final-year project from your work experience.

➡ **JOB PROSPECTS**
A recent survey found that 50 per cent of employers recruit from students who have had work experience with their organisation.
(Source: IRS Employment Review)

## ● How much do you get?

Typical rates are £1,000–2,000 a year to help towards costs of study plus £800–1,700 salary per month during work periods.

> **EFFECT ON YOUR STUDENT LOAN PACKAGE**
> **Money from a sponsor is not included in the calculation for how much Student Loan, Grant or university bursary you can have.**

## ● Who gets sponsorship?

Mostly students studying engineering, surveying and business-related subjects.

## ● Likely sponsors

• Large companies or organisations, especially those working in an area relevant to your studies. They may not advertise student sponsorship, but you may be able to make a convincing case for them to support you.

• Armed Forces.

• Ministry of Defence.

• Professional organisations such as the Institute of Engineering and Technology (IET) which awards around 60 Power Academy scholarships each year for engineering and technology students. These are offered at six universities (Cardiff, Imperial College, Strathclyde, Manchester, Southampton and Queen's Belfast) and backed by 16 companies offering sponsorship in the power industry, including Scottish & Southern Energy, Siemens and Rolls-Royce. You get a bursary of £2,200 for each year of study, a contribution towards tuition fees, £220 for books and software, mentors from the industrial partner and paid summer work placements. For more information and to download an application form, go to the IET website: www.theiet.org/poweracademy.

**SPONSORSHIP TIPS**

- Apply to a company that interests you, and one where you would like to forge your career.
- Check the training programme is what you want and accredited by the appropriate institution.
- Compare salaries and bursaries.
- Choose a location close to home or where accommodation is affordable.
- Check the small print of your contract.
- See the tips for students seeking work, page 117.

## ● How and when to apply

Apply early in your final school year and before you send in your UCAS form if you are seeking full degree course sponsorship. There may also be opportunities to get sponsorship for the second year or final year of your degree – your course tutor should have a list of sponsoring companies.

## 12   Taking a gap year

Some students take a year out between finishing at school or college and starting university, often known as a 'gap year', 'year out' or 'deferred year'. This could be a time to raise some money before going to university, but there are many other good reasons to take a gap year, including the opportunity to:

- gain experience or skills
- travel abroad
- do voluntary work
- recharge your batteries before beginning at university
- have fun, excitement and challenging experiences

In general, gap years are a good thing. It is possible to go trekking in Thailand, sailing in the Seychelles, teaching in Tanzania, on an adventure up the Amazon or even do drama in Stratford-upon-Avon. You can go for a few weeks or a full year and some opportunities will enable you to earn money to finance your degree course. If you choose your opportunity carefully, you will develop the kind of maturity and enterprise that will help with your future career, as well as your time at university. Many employers look favourably on graduates who have taken gap years, recognising that these students often acquire useful skills such as team working, fundraising and thinking under pressure. Some also become fluent in a foreign language.

On the other hand, a gap year means it will be one year later before you are in the job market after graduation and earning a salary. If your chosen course is a long one, this could be a consideration. In a few subjects it may take you a little while to get back into serious study – mathematics is notorious for being a bit harder to take up again after a year away from study – but most students soon catch up again.

## ● Planning your gap year

Planning is essential to avoid disappointment. There are a number of reputable organisations that can help you organise your gap year. They take care of some of the practicalities, have ready-made activities, and have a proper concern for safety and security. Check the links on The Complete University Guide website (www.thecompleteuniversityguide.co.uk).

The Year Out Group www.yearoutgroup.org produces a useful booklet called 'Planning your Year Out' and their website links to organisations running year-out projects in the UK or overseas; many of these you have to finance yourself, some are paid.

## ● Do I apply to university this year?

If you are thinking about taking a gap year it is still best to apply during your final year at school or college. When filling in the online application, indicate that you wish to defer for one year when you complete the Choices section. This should mean that you get your university place sorted out before starting your job or travels so you don't have to worry about it during your gap year. Indeed, for the more adventurous travellers, trying to fill in a UCAS form on the back of a

Mongolian yak or half way across the Australian desert is not recommended. Also, if things go badly wrong in your examinations and you don't get a place, you do get an opportunity to rethink your career options or resit your exams and still start at university when you planned to.

As a general rule, universities are happy to consider deferred applicants but, if the prospectus does not make a clear statement about the university's policy, it would be sensible to check.

Once you have secured your university place you can apply for student finance the following year in the normal way (see chapters 3–8).

**DEFERRING A PLACE**
According to UCAS, in 2007 some 7 per cent of applicants deferred their university places until the following year (that's 28,863 out of 413,430 applicants).

## How much could you earn during a gap year?

If you plan to work during your gap year, don't expect much more than the minimum wage – £4.77 per hour for 18–21 year-olds and £5.73 per hour for workers aged 22 and over (the last increase was in 2008). Part-time and casual staff are entitled to the national minimum wage on exactly the same terms as full-time staff, but there are some exceptions. For example, people living and working as part of a family, such as au pairs, are exempt from the minimum wage protection.

## More information

• For **jobs**, try chain stores, supermarkets, banks, insurance companies, accountancy firms – they may offer work experience and/or a training scheme. If teaching sounds attractive, you may find a role as an assistant teacher in a preparatory school. There are more suggestions for finding work in chapter 13, 'Working while you study', along with useful information about student income tax.

• For **volunteering**: see the suggestions on the website www.yearoutgroup.org. Also, take a look at the National Trust volunteering programme www.nationaltrust.org.uk/volunteer ing, BTCV conservation holidays www.btcv.org/shop and archaeological digs (for digs at home, see the magazine *British Archaeology*; for digs abroad contact Archaeology Abroad, www.britarch.ac.uk/archabroad).

• For **travel**: InterRail passes and rail passes offered by other European countries can be obtained via the Student Travel Office www.statravel.co.uk. The International Student Travel Confederation www.isic.org offers an International Youth Travel Card (IYTC) for people under 26, giving many discounts. Look for cheap deals for students on buses, coaches, trains and planes. For modestly-priced accommodation, try the Youth Hostel Association (YHA), which has places to stay worldwide (you need to be a member to use hostels in other countries – get an annual card from www.yha.org.uk). For train travel, a Young Person's Railcard is invaluable (you have to be aged 16–25 or a mature student in full-time education): it gives you a third off most UK rail fares. Coaches offer a cheap way to travel long distances: a student coachcard (for students over 17) gives you a third off National Express and Scottish Citylink fares, and some continental and Irish services – check with National Express (www.nationalexpress.com). If you want to travel abroad on an organised programme, you might consider Operation Raleigh (www.raleighinternational.org), which offers 5- or 10-week expeditions to remote places, working on community and envi-

ronmental projects as well as providing tough adventure challenges. But you'll need to raise funds beforehand – around
£3,000 for a 10-week expedition or £1,750 for 5 weeks, and that
doesn't include the cost of flights, kit or vaccinations. You may
need to apply for a visa before you go. Coral Cay Conservation
(CCC) offers volunteering and expedition opportunities to
gap-year students where you can be involved in helping to protect threatened coral reefs and tropical forests (typical costs for
a 4-week marine expedition: £1,450 excluding flights, insurance, equipment, etc). CCC offers some advice on fundraising –
check their website (www.coralcay.org).

- Google 'student gap year' for more ideas and opportunities.

---

**GAP YEAR TIPS**

- Plan your year carefully.
- Secure your university place then ask for deferment.
- Work close to home to avoid high accommodation costs.
- Working for chain stores/supermarkets might offer a transfer to a part-time job with them in your university town.
- Budget carefully and don't run up debts.
- Travel with reputable organisations.
- Take out travel and health insurance if going abroad – many companies offer student discounts, for example, www.statravel.co.uk and www.endsleigh.co.uk. See page 151 for more on insurance.

---

**Student Talk**

*'In my gap year I had a full-time job in order
to save up money for university life, which I
have been entirely reliant on so far.'*

### Student Talk

'I worked during my gap year – not the most exciting of options but it did give me the security of some extra cash to fall back on when there were unforeseen expenditures (like buying a bike to get to campus). I'd had a part-time job as a waitress, and they let me stay on full-time for a year. It's certainly not fun putting plates on tables when all your mates are back-packing across Australia or trekking in Peru – but it was a more practical option.'

'I worked hard in my gap year to save for university and then did a six-month ski season in Val d'Isère where I hosted in a chalet for 12 paying guests. Having the opportunity to ski and snowboard every day was great and I got to speak a considerable amount of French which has been helpful in my choice of degree.'

'I did a variety of paid work (call centre, admin and working as a holiday rep abroad), which allowed me to come to university with about £1,500 in savings. Due to the fact that my parents pay my rent, I am able to scrape through this year by using my loan for living costs. If I had to rely on my loan to pay my rent as well as live, I just don't know what I'd do.'

# 13  Working while you study

Many students work part-time during term time and full-time during the vacations for the simple reason that they need extra cash. Student funding from the government and other institutions in most cases isn't enough to finance you through university. Earning while you study gives you valuable work experience, as well as funds, and demonstrates to future employers that you have a responsible attitude to managing your finances. But you need to make sure that your job doesn't interfere with your studies, especially if your course is particularly demanding. Most universities suggest a limit on the number of hours a week you work during term time (usually around 15 hours maximum). Oxford and Cambridge colleges generally discourage students from taking regular paid employment or at least recommend that you consult your supervisor first. International students should check their UK visa to make sure it contains no limitation on working.

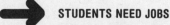

**STUDENTS NEED JOBS**

Over 40 per cent of undergraduates will have to work to make ends meet while they are at university.

## ● Vacation work

Also known as 'placements', 'work experience' and 'internships', vacation work covers virtually every job you can imagine, from strawberry picking in Dorset to managing a project for a PR company in Paris. You may be lucky enough to find a job that leads to full-time employment after graduation or teaches you skills useful for your career. Even if your job is temporary or casual, make sure you are paid at least the minimum wage (page 107).

➡ **SUMMER WORKERS**
According to a recent survey, 86 per cent of students in their second year of study and above work during the summer vacation.

### Student Talk

*'I worked during the summer vacation cleaning holiday cottages. I got paid above the minimum wage and didn't have to deal with customers! It would be a good idea to ring or email holiday parks or holiday home rental companies as they need extra staff in the summer.'*

*'In the vacations I work as a bellydancer – a bit more unusual than most summer jobs, but a great way to earn money doing something I love.'*

## ● Part-time term work

Part-time jobs during term time can really help your finances. For many students, they are necessary for survival. The best part-time jobs are easily accessible, fit in with your study schedule, pay well and give you useful work experience and skills. By far the simplest option is to work on the university site – jobs vary from library assistant to bar work in the Students' Union. You may have more choice if you look further afield, but don't forget to factor in any travel costs and the time getting there.

### AVERAGE WEEKLY EARNINGS AND HOURS WORKED BY STUDENTS

| University town | Average weekly earnings | Average hours worked per week |
|---|---|---|
| Brighton | £120 | 15 |
| Plymouth | £115 | 18 |
| Bristol | £107 | 14 |
| London | £103 | 15 |
| Belfast | £102 | 15 |
| Aberdeen | £99 | 17 |
| Newcastle | £92 | 14 |
| Lancaster | £88 | 12 |
| Cardiff | £85 | 14 |
| Edinburgh | £76 | 12 |
| Sheffield | £75 | 14 |
| Birmingham | £72 | 10 |
| York | £65 | 12 |
| Southampton | £59 | 11 |

(Source: NatWest Student Living Index 2008)

If you're wondering how much students earn, the table on the previous page shows average weekly earnings and hours worked by students in a range of university towns. Brighton students earn the most at £120 a week on average but Aberdeen students work the longest hours at 17 hours per week. Southampton students work much less, and earn less: £59 a week on average.

**JOB TIPS**

- Allow yourself time to unwind and relax after work or study.
- Keep a diary and try to stick to structured work patterns so you know when your course assignments are due, when you will work on them and when you are due to work on your job.
- Try to cut back on your part-time work during exam periods.
- If you can't cope with the workload, speak to your course tutor and employer at once as they may be able to suggest practical solutions.

---

### Student Talk

*'Don't work too many hours – it will affect your degree.'*

---

## Where to look for work

- For **part-time or temporary work** during term time, contact your university Job Shop, the service set up with the specific aim of finding work for students during term time and vacations. The Job Shop will have lists of student-friendly vacancies, with staff who can advise you on finding work to fit in with your course. For details of your local Job Shop, check the Job Shop listings at the following website: http://targetjob.co.uk/job-hunting-tools/university-job-shops.aspx. The National Association of Student Employment Services (NASES) website gives useful information on topics such as employment rights, work permits for international students, how to combine work and study (www.nases.org.uk).

• For **vacation work**, if you plan to go home or live in another part of the country, you can find details of Job Shops across the country that are open during the vacations through the NASES Vacation Link scheme (www.nases.org.uk under 'Nases' – 'Vacation Link').

• For **work placements or work experience**, see pages 80–2. Organisations often advertise in university careers services. Try the work experience and graduate employment websites through the 'Links' section at www.thecompleteuniversityguide.co.uk. Student work websites include: www.prospects.ac.uk (Prospects – graduate careers website); www.e4s.co.uk; www.work-experience.org (National Council for Work Experience); www.justjobs4students.co.uk; www.student-part-time.jobs.com; www.activate.co.uk; www.yougofurther.co.uk.

 **STUDENT WORK FACTS**

• The number of students working part-time during term time is rapidly increasing: nearly 25,000 more undergraduates took up part-time employment in 2008 than in 2007.

• On average, students work 14 hours per week on their part-time jobs, although a quarter of students work more than 20 hours.

(Source: NatWest Student Living Index 2008).

Try also:

- Temping agencies and local employment agencies.
- Job advertisements in local newspapers, shop windows and supermarket noticeboards. You could advertise your skills locally as a proof reader, tutor or translator, etc.
- Local businesses and organisations requiring temporary clerical staff.
- Cafés, restaurants and bars requiring bar staff, waiters and waitresses.
- Construction companies requiring labourers.
- Shops requiring sales assistants during the Christmas season.
- Tourist attractions requiring guides or ticket sellers.
- Mail order companies for packing jobs.
- Farms for seasonal work, for example, fruit picking.
- Hotels, chalets and restaurants in ski and other resorts requiring hospitality workers.
- Summer camps which recruit students for work during vacations, for example, Eurocamp (www.summerjobs4u.co.uk/Eurocamp.htm). Bunac in America offers summer camp work and also a work experience programme (Work America) that guides you through the process of securing a working visa and finding employment in the USA, whether you are looking for summer jobs, casual work while travelling or career-related work experience (www.bunac.org/uk/workamerica).

**DO YOUR EARNINGS AFFECT YOUR STUDENT LOAN?**
Money earned during vacations or from part-time work during term time is not included in the calculation for how much Student Loan, grant or university bursary you can have. However, other income you have during the academic year may be taken into account, for example, bank or building society interest, certain social security benefits or even a pension!

## JOB SEARCH TIPS

- Don't leave job finding until the last minute – competition is high especially over vacations. You need to start thinking about summer vacation work just after Christmas.
- Brush up on your languages if you plan to work abroad.
- Make sure your CV is professional and up-to-date.
- Your initial approach needs to be concise and tailored to the needs or aims of the organisation you are contacting. Try to obtain a contact name if you are applying for work which is not advertised. A generic letter to a 'Dear Sir/Madam' or to the chief executive is unlikely to get anywhere.
- Highlight your relevant skills, experience and what you can offer the organisation.
- Dress appropriately for interview and sell yourself!

### Student Talk

*'I make the odd bit of pocket money by participating in psychology experiments on campus. It's not a regular income – a fiver or so here and there – but it's flexible and usually quite fun. I've been paid to drink alcohol and even to test ice cream!'*

*'Working as a student rep is a great way to earn money – you walk around campus all day telling people all about your uni, and get a free lunch. It's normally on a Wednesday or Saturday, which is perfect if you're not part of a sports club.'*

**Student Talk**

*'I work in a bar. I just handed in my CV to as many places as possible and took what I was offered.'*

*'As I managed to get a job I have been able to pay off two-thirds of my overdraft, so getting a job is pretty important.'*

*'I work as a Student Ambassador for the university. This job is pretty much perfect for me and I would definitely recommend it. I can balance work around when I have lectures/coursework and there is no pressure to work. It pays quite well, and I love it! It doesn't really feel like work because you basically share your life experiences and show people what your university is about.'*

## Student income tax

As a student you are not exempt from paying tax. Although you don't pay tax on your Student Loan, grant or bursary, you will have to declare your earnings to the HM Revenue & Customs (HMRC) from any part-time job or vacation work.

The income tax system in the UK can be complicated for students, especially if you have more than one job or work in the holidays. If you're on a tight student budget, the last thing you want is to pay too much tax and not know how to claim a refund, so it's worth getting to know the basics of the tax system.

## Tax basics

There are two taxes on your earned income: Income tax and National Insurance Contributions (NIC). Your National Insurance Contributions build up your right to claim social security in the future (for example, a state pension and unemployment benefit). They are calculated and deducted on a monthly basis according to what you earn, and cannot be claimed back once paid. Income tax is a compulsory contribution to the government, to help finance public services such as the NHS, education and defence. The amount you pay depends on your annual, rather than monthly, earnings.

When you begin employment you must always supply your National Insurance Number (NINo) to your employer. Based on information about your income and entitlement to allowances, the Tax Office will issue you a tax code, which will tell your employer how much tax to deduct from your wages before you get paid. The amount deducted will appear on your payslip, usually marked 'PAYE' (Pay as You Earn), which is the name of this scheme for paying tax. The employer will then pay the tax directly to HMRC.

You only pay tax on your earnings over a certain threshold, known as your 'Personal Allowance' – in the tax year 6 April 2009 to 5 April 2010, the personal allowance is £6,475. In other words, if you earn less than £6,475 (around £124 a week) you will not pay any tax. As soon as you earn over this threshold, deductions will be made from your earnings.

If you have never worked before, you may be placed on an emergency tax code, which automatically taxes you while your employer waits for information from the HMRC about your tax code status. If you have worked before, when you left your last job you should have been given a form P45, which shows your earnings in the tax year and how much tax was deducted. Give the P45 to your next employer. At the end of the tax year (which runs from 6 April one year to 5 April the next), if you are still working for the same employer you should receive a form P60, which is a summary of your earnings and any tax that has been deducted from them during the tax year.

### TAX TIPS

- Always keep your payslips and forms P45 and P60. You may need them as evidence when you are dealing with the HMRC.
- Be wary of working for employers who refuse to give you a payslip or record you on the payroll or only pay in cash. They are breaking the law.
- Keep a check on your tax records and claim a refund for any excess tax paid.

## Paying too much tax

In general, if you have a part-time job throughout the year then the PAYE scheme should calculate your income tax correctly. However, students often work for only part of the tax year, which can lead to overpayment of tax. For example, if you have a summer job for 10 weeks and you earn £200 a week, you will earn £2,000 – which is less than the £6,475 tax threshold so you shouldn't pay tax if these are the only earnings you have all year. But the PAYE system deducts income tax monthly on the basis that you would go on earning £200 a month all year, equivalent to a salary of £10,400 – which is more than the tax threshold so PAYE automatically deducts the tax.

You can also pay too much tax if you were put on the wrong tax code or just started a new job and had an emergency tax code for a while.

## How to claim back overpaid tax

Use the Inland Revenue Student Tax Checker at www.hmrc.gov.uk/calcs/stc.htm to check if you've paid too much tax. There are several ways to get your overpaid tax back:

• This can be automatic if you are on the company's payroll and continuing work into the following year, or if you take on a new job within four weeks of leaving the old one. Your tax refund should automatically be included with your wages in the following weeks/months. However, if you think you are still paying too much tax, tell your employer's Tax Office why and they will say which documents you need to send.

• If your job is temporary, you should ask your employer for a form P45 when you finish the job. You can claim a tax rebate after four weeks of leaving if you have returned to your studies. You'll need to fill in a form P50 'Claiming tax back when you have stopped working', and take this to your Tax Office, together with your P45.

## Avoid paying too much tax

The good news is that you can avoid paying too much tax by following a few simple steps:

• Avoid being put on an emergency tax code (and paying the wrong amount of tax) by making sure you get a P45 from your employer when you leave a job so you can give it to your next employer.

• Complete a form P38S 'Student Employees' if you are unlikely to earn more than the £6,475 threshold during the tax year. Give the form to your employer before you start work to stop any tax deductions from your wages.

• You can stop your bank or building society deducting tax on any interest you earn on your bank or building society account by completing a form R85 and giving it to the bank, but you need to be confident that your earned income won't exceed £6,475 during the tax year. This is worth doing if you have a reasonable sum of money in a savings account, for example your Tuition Fee Loan and Maintenance Loan. There's no point paying tax unnecessarily! If in doubt as to whether your bank or building society interest can be paid without tax taken off, use the Inland Revenue checker at www.hmrc.gov.uk/calcs/r85.

All the forms mentioned above can be downloaded from HMRC (www.hmrc.gov.uk) or collected from your local tax office.

 **NO TAX TO PAY ON STUDENT FUNDING**
Your Student Loan, grants and gifts from parents or friends do not count towards the tax thresholds. You only pay income tax on earned income!

## More information
For further details on tax codes and the PAYE system, and for information about tax self-assessment for self-employed workers, visit the HMRC website: www.hmrc.gov.uk, or for specific information relating to students: www.hmrc.gov.uk/students.

## European and international students – UK tax
If you intend to work while studying in the UK you will need a National Insurance Number so that your employer can pay

your wages and make any applicable income tax or National Insurance deductions. UK residents are allocated a number automatically at the age of 16, but as a non-UK European or International student you will need to apply for one by contacting the National Insurance Office (telephone 0845 600 0643) and booking an application interview. The interview will usually be held at your local Job Centre Plus. You should take certain documents with you, including your passport and confirmation of your student status (for example, an admissions letter from the university) and proof of your UK address.

For general information about working in the UK visit the UK Council for International Student Affairs (UKCISA) website: www.ukcisa.org.uk, or contact their advice line: outside the UK, +44 20 7107 9922; inside the UK, 020 7107 9922.

# PART 3: EXPENDITURE

How much is it going to cost you to be a student? This part of the book is about the tuition fees for your course and all the day-to-day living expenses that you will incur, including accommodation. There are also tips on how to manage your money.

## 14   Tuition fees

Tuition fees have been introduced in all four countries of the UK (England, Northern Ireland, Scotland and Wales) but not all students will have to pay them (see Scotland – below). They are often known as 'top-up fees' because the amount students pay does not represent the full cost of the tuition, only a proportion. These were first introduced by a narrow vote in the UK Parliament and set at a maximum of £3,000 for students going to university in 2006. It was agreed that this could increase in line with inflation and that there would be a review after the academic year 2009/10. It looks as if that review will be announced late in 2009 but will not report until after the General Election expected in 2010.

### ● Key facts

• In England, Northern Ireland and Wales, universities can charge different (variable) fees for different courses up to a maximum level set by the government. In practice, the vast majority charge the maximum, which is £3,225 for 2009/10, but a few do charge less. For example, Greenwich charges £2,900 rather than the full £3,225, and Leeds Metropolitan £2,000.

• Full-time UK and other EU undergraduate students don't have to pay the fees upfront: you can get a **Tuition Fee Loan** to cover the full fees and you don't have to repay the loan until you've finished your studies and are earning more than £15,000 (page 16).

•    Scottish students studying full-time in Scotland have their fees paid for them by the SAAS but this is not done automatically – you will still have to make an application each year (see below).

•    The government cap on tuition fees may well be raised, but this would be only likely to affect students starting their courses after 2010. For further news on this, check your student finance provider website.

# ● How much do you have to pay?

## a) UK and other EU students
### Studying in England, Wales and Northern Ireland

The maximum tuition fee in 2009/10 for full-time undergraduates is £3,225 a year. Universities have the option of varying the fees for different courses but in the vast majority of cases they charge the maximum – check the websites below for details, or the university's prospectus. You can apply for a **Tuition Fee Loan** to cover the full fee charged by your university. Expect your tuition fees to increase each year in line with inflation.

**WEBLINKS: TUITION FEES**

•    For tuition fees at UK institutions look under the course search on the UCAS website (www.ucas.com). From here you can access links to the relevant university webpages.

•    For tuition fees at English institutions only, use the Student Finance Calculator at www.direct.gov.uk/studentfinance.

•    For comparing fees at a glance, try the listing at www.publicgoods.co.uk (click on Education, then select fees download).

## Studying in Scotland

Unlike the rest of the UK, tuition fees do not vary between institutions in Scotland. There is a fixed fee of £1,820 for most degree courses (£2,895 for medicine), but these fees only affect students coming to Scottish universities from other parts of the UK. If you are one of these students, you can (as any other student in the rest of the UK) defer payment of your fees by applying for a **Tuition Fee Loan** administered by the student finance provider for your home country. Those of you who are ordinarily resident in Scotland and plan to stay there to study full-time for an undergraduate degree can have your fees paid for you by the SAAS, but this is not done automatically – you will still have to apply each academic year. The SAAS will also pay the fees of non-UK EU students on application. (Scottish students studying in England, Wales and Northern Ireland miss out on the no tuition fees policy: they pay the same fees as other UK/EU students but can take out Tuition Fee Loans to cover them.) Go to www.saas.gov.uk for more information.

### UK TUITION FEES BY COUNTRY, 2009/10

| Country | Fee level | Fee type |
|---|---|---|
| England | £3,225 (max) | Variable |
| Northern Ireland | £3,225 (max) | Variable |
| Wales | £3,225 (max) | Variable |
| Scotland | £1,820 | Fixed |
| Scotland (Medicine) | £2,895 | Fixed |

## b) International (non-EU) students

Fees for international students are not regulated by the UK government, and as such are much higher than those for 'home'

**MONEY TIP**

You must make sure you
have sufficient funds to
cover the full tuition
fees and all necessary
living costs before
leaving home.

students. These 'overseas fees' will be determined by the UK institution you plan to attend. Contact the university for more information (the fees are listed on many university websites – see the weblinks on page 128). For general information about international fees, visit the UK Council for International Student Affairs (UKCISA) website: www.ukcisa.org.uk.

### FULL-TIME INTERNATIONAL STUDENT FEES AT UK UNIVERSITIES, 2008/09

| Full-time undergraduate degree | Classroom-based courses | Laboratory or workshop based courses | Pre-clinical programmes | Clinical medicine | Clinical dentistry |
|---|---|---|---|---|---|
| Annual overseas fees charged (average) | £9,000 | £10,700 | £12,900 | £22,100 | £22,700 |

(Source: UUK survey based on data from 91 institutions.)

**FEE TIP**

Try and estimate how
much the fees are
likely to increase over
the length of your
course.

### c) UK Part-time students

Your university decides how much to charge in fees for part-time courses; there is no maximum or minimum amount set by the government. Contact the universities direct for more information. See page 76 for details of means-tested grants available to help you pay your tuition fees.

## 15   Living costs

For all students, the biggest expenditure items during their stay at university are the regular living costs such as accommodation, food and drink, travel, perhaps even some new clothes, plus any course-related costs such as books and equipment. There is much evidence to suggest that most university entrants don't know what it costs to be a student and can seriously underestimate their expenditure by as much as 50 per cent.

Where you choose to study can affect your living costs. If you are planning to get a part-time job, Plymouth is the most cost-effective place in the UK for undergraduates to study, according to the NatWest Student Living Index 2008. The index puts Plymouth at the top because of its attractive combination of low average living and accommodation costs and the potential to earn reasonable money from part-time work. NatWest

### COST OF LIVING

Most students struggle to pay for the basics they need to survive. Although the price of many non-food goods is currently falling in the economic recession, the British Retail Consortium found that food prices remain high and are still increasing – at an annual rate of around 6 per cent at the beginning of 2009. This presents a problem for students because food accounts for a large amount of weekly outgoings.

interviewed 100 students at 26 university towns to come up
with its findings – not a full coverage of all university towns
but it does illustrate how you might be better off financially
living in some towns rather than others. The rankings were
worked out as follows: average local weekly student expenditure on living and accommodation was divided by average
local weekly income for working students, giving a differen-
tial value which was then used to rank the university towns.
The rankings are shown opposite (with the previous year's
rankings in brackets).

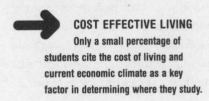

**COST EFFECTIVE LIVING**
Only a small percentage of
students cite the cost of living and
current economic climate as a key
factor in determining where they study.

The research found
that Plymouth students
spend on average £217
per week on living and
housing costs, but they
manage to offset these
costs in part with impressive weekly earnings of £115 from part-
time work. In Exeter, by contrast, students spend £294 per week on
average but earn just £67 from term-time employment.

## ● Accommodation

An increasing number of students, particularly in
London, decide to live at home and travel daily to a
nearby university, and this is probably the cheapest way to
get through university. But if you decide to live away from
home, then your accommodation costs will be your largest
expense.

In the table on page 135, which compares average weekly student rents in 26 university towns, London comes out as the

## NATWEST STUDENT LIVING INDEX 2008: RANKINGS FOR 26 UNIVERSITY TOWNS

| Ranking (no. 1 is top of the league table) | University town |
|---|---|
| 1 | Plymouth (*) |
| 2 | Cambridge (13) |
| 3 | Dundee (3) |
| 4 | Brighton (2) |
| 5 | Portsmouth |
| 6 | Bristol (9) |
| 7 | Leeds (1) |
| 8 | Liverpool (5) |
| 9 | Belfast (19) |
| 10 | Aberdeen (18) |
| 11 | Newcastle (10) |
| 12 | Sheffield (11) |
| 13 | Glasgow (8) |
| 14 | London (4) |
| 15 | Nottingham (27) |
| 16 | Lancaster (25) |
| 17 | Cardiff (16) |
| 18 | Edinburgh (23) |
| 19 | York (21) |
| 20 | Leicester (6) |
| 21 | Oxford (24) |
| 22 | Birmingham (7) |
| 23 | Swansea (*) |
| 24 | Manchester (15) |
| 25 | Southampton (26) |
| 26 | Exeter (*) |

* University town was not included in the previous year's research.

most expensive place with an average rent of £103. Liverpool, Lancaster, Belfast, Dundee, Birmingham and Swansea look reasonable by comparison, with student rents ranging from £53 to £57 a week. The figures are provided by accommodationfor students.com.

## Living in your parents' home

One of the consequences of rising levels of student debt is that more students are choosing to live at home with their parents and study at a nearby university. Currently, 22 per cent of all students live with their parents or guardians and this figure rises to 40 per cent amongst low-income families. For many, the main disadvantage of living at home is that you miss out on some of the social life that occurs in halls of residence or shared student houses. On the other hand you may have fewer financial worries and fewer distractions when you want to get down to some decent study.

## University halls of residence

These are usually the most popular form of accommodation for first-year undergraduates as you can get to know other students living in the same halls. In most cases the halls are situated centrally on campus, so everyday travel costs should be minimal. The environment is normally safe with proper security systems; some accommodation packages even offer possessions insurance, but make sure the cover is adequate for your needs (page 151). You can choose between self-catering and full catering – the latter may be expensive but then you spend less in the supermarket. It's common for rental charges to include Internet access, and you won't have to pay utility bills (gas, electricity, water) on top. There are other benefits too, such as having your linen washed once a week and the bathrooms cleaned regularly – a big bonus for

## COMPARING AVERAGE WEEKLY RENTS

| University town | Average weekly rent |
| --- | --- |
| London | £103 |
| Cambridge | £86 |
| Exeter | £82 |
| Brighton | £81 |
| Oxford | £75 |
| Edinburgh | £71 |
| Glasgow | £70 |
| Bristol | £69 |
| Portsmouth | £69 |
| Plymouth | £67 |
| Leeds | £62 |
| Newcastle | £62 |
| Nottingham | £62 |
| York | £62 |
| Aberdeen | £61 |
| Southampton | £61 |
| Cardiff | £59 |
| Manchester | £58 |
| Sheffield | £58 |
| Leicester | £57 |
| Swansea | £57 |
| Birmingham | £56 |
| Dundee | £54 |
| Belfast | £53 |
| Lancaster | £53 |
| Liverpool | £53 |

(Source: accommodationforstudents.com April 2009)

many students! The contract is usually for term time only (30–40 weeks a year), so you won't be paying for a room unnecessarily if you go home or away during the vacations.

## Private rented accommodation

Many students opt to move out of university halls of residence in their second year, once they've met a group of friends who want to share a house with them. Living away from campus and sharing with friends can have many benefits, in particular the camaraderie and friendship that often develops when people live together; it can also have its downsides when personalities clash and the accommodation is squalid and poorly maintained.

You'll have to negotiate the length of your tenancy with a private landlord. Most landlords prefer a twelve-month contract but this will mean you have to pay for accommodation during the vacations, when you may well be elsewhere – can you afford it? Try to negotiate a tenancy agreement for the exact time that you want. One way to achieve this is to include a break clause in the contract, which allows either you or the landlord to give two months' notice to end the tenancy after six months. Find out what's included in the rent. You may have to pay utility bills and Internet access on top. In case you cause damage to the property or its contents, you will normally be required to pay a deposit, which should be returned to you at the end of the tenancy. The usual amount is one calendar month's rent.

If the accommodation is not within walking distance of the campus, you should check the availability of public transport, particularly late at night. Make sure the area is well lit and relatively safe, especially after dark, and that the house is secure –

many insurance companies insist upon five-lever dead locks on
the external doors and window locks on the ground floor.

Ideally you should have:

• **a tenancy agreement**, which is good protection for you
and contains details such as the length of the agreement, the
rent payable, and what is and isn't allowed in the property. It
may also set out, for example, what kind of repairs the landlord
should make and by when, the procedures for ending the tenancy, and how the landlord may increase the rent. Most con-
tracts for private rented accommodation will be **Assured
Shorthold Tenancies** (this is the automatic or default tenancy
created between a landlord letting a residential property in
England or Wales to a tenant for between six months and three
years). You can download a guide for tenants of Assured
Shorthold Tenancies at www.communities.gov.uk/publica
tions/housing/assuredassuredtenants. If you are sharing a large
house of three or more storeys with five or more students (a
'**house in multiple occupation**'), you may have a 'bare contrac-
tual tenancy'. Houses in multiple occupation must be licensed
with the local council. Such licences are intended as a protective
measure for tenants and are only granted to landlords if certain
minimum facilities are provided and the building is kept in a
good state of repair. If you are a **lodger** living in a house with
your landlord you may simply have a verbal agreement or
licence. Make sure you are aware of your rights under your particular contract. For information on tenancy agreements and
landlords' obligations in each country of the UK, check the
housing section in the Citizens Advice online guide at
www.adviceguide.org.uk.

• **an inventory** of the contents and condition of the property at the commencement of your tenancy. Ask the landlord

for an inventory, which you should check for accuracy. If the landlord doesn't provide one then make one yourself when you arrive at the property – a set of photographs is ideal. Send a copy to the landlord by 'recorded signed for' post in case there's a dispute at the end of the tenancy with regard to the return of your deposit.

If you have an Assured Shorthold Tenancy you will automatically have:

• **Tenancy Deposit Protection** (TDP), which will stop your landlord from unfairly withholding your deposit when you leave. This deposit protection is a result of recent legislation in England and Wales aimed at Assured Shorthold Tenancies. Within 14 days of receiving your deposit your landlord or the letting agent must inform you of how the deposit has been protected under one of the approved schemes. A free dispute resolution service is provided with the scheme – see www.direct.gov.uk/en/TenancyDeposit/index.htm for details. Scotland has passed the law to bring in TDP but hasn't yet confirmed whether it will be introduced. There are other schemes in place to protect tenants in Scotland, for example, to ensure that properties are 'fit and proper' for letting (see www.better rentingscotland.com). Currently TDP doesn't apply in Northern Ireland, but different legislation has been introduced to help ensure properties are fit to let. Check the 'landlord and tenant obligations' at www.nidirect.gov.uk/index/property-and-housing/ buying-selling-and-renting-a-home/letting-your-property or ask at your University Accommodation Office for details.

You should also (by law) be given:
• A copy of the **Gas Safety certificate** before you move into the property, which confirms that a suitably qualified engineer

who is listed on the Gas Safe Register (formerly CORGI, the Council for Registered Gas Installers) has checked all gas appliances and flues in the property for safety within twelve months of installation and thereafter at least every twelve months.

## RENTING TIPS

- Don't be in a rush to take the first place you are offered – consider several alternatives and weigh up the pros and cons of each. Avoid renting far away from university unless rents are significantly lower and transport is cheap and frequent (check the times of the last bus at night).
- Go back after dark to see if the area feels safe for walking home at night (taking taxis can be expensive).
- Areas with large numbers of students have social benefits but can make rich pickings for burglars. If there have been many break-ins in the area then your insurance costs will be higher.
- When viewing properties, ask to see the Energy Performance Certificate, which landlords must now provide for tenants. You will then be able to see how energy efficient the property is and how this may affect your household bills.
- Living with non-students: make sure they are aware that full-time students are largely exempt from paying Council Tax and you won't therefore be contributing to this cost. (Part-time students are not exempt from paying Council Tax.)
- You will only need one TV licence if your house is rented on a shared basis, but if you have an individual tenancy for your room with a shared communal area then you will need a licence for each TV in the house. You can claim a pro-rata refund on your TV licence if you go home for the summer vacation.
- Make sure your fellow tenants know about the terms of the tenancy – the rent they must pay, by when and the length of the tenancy. To avoid arguments over paying the rent, set up individual standing orders for each tenant directly into the landlord's or letting agent's bank account.
- Agree with fellow tenants how bills will be shared from the outset. Keep a house kitty which everyone contributes to each week to cover essentials (bills, toilet rolls, cleaning equipment, tea, coffee, sugar, etc) and breakages.

**Student Talk**

'I am a first year so I live in halls because it's the most common thing to do. I am paying £139 per week, which is such a huge amount to pay and if I could do it over again I would choose cheaper accommodation.'

'I applied for en-suite accommodation but ended up in a house with shared bathroom facilities. I am glad that I was put in this accommodation as I have saved around £25 a week, and I never have a problem waiting for the bathroom. I currently pay £82.50 a week.'

'I opted for a quiet flat so that I'd be able to get some sleep! I was paying £101 a week, which put a massive dent in my finances, but it was worth it… This year I live in a shared house with the same people from last year, and we pay £80 a week, which is expensive in terms of the UK, but we're in Brighton.'

'By self-catering you can eat what you want, when you want at your own convenience and you don't feel as though you have lost money by eating out as the food is still going to be in the fridge when you get home. The cost of all bills and broadband Internet is included in my £3,181 a year (roughly £80 x 39 weeks) hall fees.

## Where to find accommodation

• The University Accommodation Office for places in halls of residence and local landlords and letting agents for privately owned accommodation. The Student Accommodation Manager will provide help and advice.

• University web pages with information about university accommodation (specifications, rents, etc). These can be accessed via www.thecompleteuniversityguide.co.uk – go to 'Profiles' and search for the relevant UK institution from the navigation bar on the left. Each university profile has an accommodation entry with a link to the university accommodation website. Also, check the 'Links' (student accommodation) on the same website. Here you'll find sites such as www.accommo dationforstudents.com – a search engine for UK student accommodation, including private accommodation.

• UNITE (www.unite-students.com) is the largest provider of student accommodation in the UK. They house over 39,000 students in 126 properties across 33 towns and cities. There are no hidden costs: Internet access, contents insurance and household bills are included in the rent. You can choose from a studio or a flat to share with up to seven friends at a range of prices. Register on the website and you can view the accommodation on line.

• UNIAID Foundation (www.uniaid.org.uk) – the Foyer UNIAID Accommodation Bursary scheme can provide a year's free accommodation. See their website for details.

• A letting agent in a high street residential lettings office can help to find suitable properties but may charge an administration fee (around £20–30) to obtain references for you, which are then passed on to the landlord. You can find letting agents by checking 'To let' boards outside local properties or via an Internet search.

- Private rented accommodation is often advertised in local papers and newsagents' windows.

---

**Student Talk**

*'Make sure everybody sees the house, and if you can, try to talk to some of the current tenants when the landlord isn't there. They can tell you all the stuff he won't: what it's really like, the fact that the boiler is really loud at night or that the shower is rubbish, and even more importantly, what the landlord's like.'*

*'Don't be lured into the panic that always happens when the student accommodation lists go up. Yes, it is good to get in there early if you can, but really don't stress over it. I was so convinced that everybody else had a house but that we were going to be homeless – yet there were still houses being advertised months into the new academic year!'*

*'Take a walk from the accommodation to uni to see if you are ready to go that distance every day to lectures.'*

---

**Further information**

Check out the Student's Guide to Private Rented Accommodation at www.mypropertyguide.co.uk (the link at the top left-hand corner of the web page). Here you'll find a useful Viewing Checklist (things to look out for when you visit a property to let), information on tenancy agreements, deposits and regulations, and how to choose your housemates and live in harmony with them.

### MONEY-SAVING TIPS

- Turn off lights in empty rooms.
- Turn down the room thermostat by one or two degrees – it can save pounds off your heating bill.
- In winter, work in the university library so you can leave the heating off at home.
- Close curtains at night to keep warmth inside.
- Use energy saving light bulbs.
- Don't leave TVs, computers and DVD/CD players on standby.
- Turn off mobile phone chargers when not in use.
- Change your energy supplier for a better deal. According to the uSwitch.com report 2007, UK students could save up to £200 a year on their electricity and gas bills by choosing the right supplier.
- Pay by direct debit to avoid late payment charges.

### Student Talk

'Live with like-minded people. If you're thinking about living with a friend, bear in mind their lifestyle. They might be fun to go out with but would you want them to be around constantly? If you prefer to study and get an early night, don't live with a party animal.'

'We have a cleaning rota which saves so many arguments. It's also a good idea to have a kitty for communal items like loo roll and cleaning products – we pay 50p a week into the pot, which is plenty.'

**Student Talk**

'I live in a house that I share with four other people. It costs about £77 a week, plus we all pay £25 a month to our landlord for bills. It's a great system – he pays all the bills out of that money, so we haven't got to worry about it, and then shows us the accounts and gives back any leftovers.'

'If you have lots of arguments about washing up, it's worth buying a set of plastic washing-up bowls in different colours. Everyone puts their dirty plates in their own bowl, then there are no pans left unclaimed for weeks on end and you can see the kitchen surfaces again!'

'You might get lazy housemates but you have to be tolerant and just be ready to clean up after they mess up the place.'

'If you're moving into halls, you just end up with who you end up with! I started a group on Facebook for people living in the same accommodation as me, which allowed everybody to find out who their flatmates were and have a chat before we even got to university.'

## ● Food

Feeding yourself is perhaps the last thing on your mind when you arrive at university, and many students under-estimate this cost. Food is usually the next highest living cost after accommodation. Your food bills (for eating in and out) can very soon spiral out of control if you don't keep a careful check on spending.

**HEALTHY TIP**

Keeping to a low budget doesn't mean you can't cook healthily and get the recommended five fresh fruit and veg a day. It's worth investing in a basic recipe book aimed at students who want healthy and satisfying dishes on a low budget with minimal kitchen equipment to hand, such as *How to Boil an Egg* by Jan Arkless (another book in the Right Way series by Constable & Robinson, £5.99).

## Confidence in the kitchen

Eating out, even simple snacks and meals on campus, soon adds up and buying ready-made food is expensive. You can make savings by learning how to cook one or two straightforward dishes. For example, a quick pasta sauce made from tinned tomatoes with a spoonful of olive oil and crushed garlic tastes good and costs half the amount of a ready-made pasta sauce.

## Food shopping on a budget

Knowing where to buy good ingredients is part of eating well, so find out where other food-loving students buy their food. Supermarkets are usually good for staples such as pasta, rice,

**WEEKLY FOOD BILLS**

Each person spends £28.42* a week on average in supermarkets in the UK, based on the findings of the official magazine for the UK grocery market, *The Grocer*. Asda is consistently the cheapest supermarket in Britain, and Morrisons usually comes second, but if you plan to switch supermarkets remember to factor in travel costs. Reduce bills by buying value branded items and looking out for special offers – the best are usually in the middle aisles.

(*Based on average weekly spending, Jan–May 2009, on a basket of typical items such as bread, coffee, fruit and veg, cereals, dairy and meat.)

noodles, tinned tuna, milk, baked beans and bread, but fresh fruit, vegetables, herbs and spices may be cheaper in a local market or from a small independent shop. Soy sauce (where would your stir-fry be without it?) is often cheaper in an ethnic store than in a regular supermarket. When you do shop in the supermarket, loose vegetables are usually priced lower than pre-packed ones, and budget ranges are often better value than well-known brands.

## FOOD TIPS

- Fix a weekly limit for spending in the supermarket and stick to it, for example £25.
- Shop in local markets for fish, fresh fruit and vegetables.
- Avoid spending money on drinks and snacks when you're out and about; carry some sandwiches, a thermos and fruit snacks instead.
- Eat jacket potatoes with different toppings.
- Get to enjoy pasta.
- Invite friends to contribute ingredients and then cook together, rather than eat out. It will save you money and you'll spend quality time with your friends.
- Invest in a student recipe book full of healthy recipes using inexpensive ingredients. Or download free recipes from the Internet.
- Write menus for the week so you can plan what you need to buy to save on shopping trips.
- Plan to make enough food for two meals.
- Plan meals using left-overs rather than throwing food away.
- Organise a food money kitty with friends and buy food in bulk to stretch your money further.
- Some shops and supermarkets are much cheaper than others – shop around.
- Go to the supermarket towards the end of the day when prices are reduced on items about to go out of date.
- If you really hate cooking, look for a part-time job where meals are included.

### Student Talk

*'Cook a huge pot of pasta sauce or soup and freeze or refrigerate the rest – or cook too much pasta and take it with you cold for lunch the next day.'*

*'As a vegetarian I enjoy fresh food, so I often go to the market at the weekend to buy my fresh fruit and veg – it's much cheaper than the supermarket and it supports the local economy.'*

*'Don't compromise when it comes to food! You can cut down on going out or some other aspect, but you need good food inside you to concentrate and do well in your studies.'*

*'Make sandwiches and take them with you to uni – you'll save so much more money, as buying lunch on campus can quickly get expensive. A prepacked sandwich costs about £2 – you could buy a loaf and a half of bread for that price!'*

*'A good way to save money is to shop online to find the food deals and split the delivery cost between your flatmates.'*

*'I spend about £40 every two weeks on food. Buy the basic/value stuff – it may not be packaged as nicely but a lot of it still tastes the same and you save money.'*

● **Travel**

The best way to save on everyday travel costs is to walk or cycle, and for many students these are their two main ways of getting about. When you do use public transport, perhaps between home and university at the beginning and end of term, or to get to campus each day if you live a fair distance away, there are ways to save money. Take advantage of the many discounts available by travelling at off peak times and (especially for trains) booking well in advance. Often there are special rates for students, but you'll need a rail card or a student identity card to qualify (page 108).

If you're wondering whether to use a bike or a car at university, compare the typical costs in the table opposite.

**TRAVEL TIPS**

- Take travel costs into account when choosing accommodation.
- Walk (if safe) or cycle.
- Use taxis only when there is no other choice.
- Book ahead for the best deals on trains.
- Use student discount cards and travel at offpeak times.
- Share car fuel costs by travelling with other students.

**Student Talk**

'The university offers a great student safety bus which only costs £1 to take students back from nights out at the Union, so we save a lot of money in terms of taxis.'

## COMPARING BIKE AND CAR COSTS

|  | Bike | Car |
|---|---|---|
| Insurance | Around £30 a year for UK only and a bike valued under £250. More for a valuable bike, but do you want to risk taking an expensive bike to university? | Many insurance companies will charge very high premiums of £1,500–2,000 a year or more for drivers aged 18–21 years. Prices depend on where the car will be used, the make, model and age of the car, etc. |
| Lock | £15–30 depending on the strength of the lock. You may need a secondary lock to secure quick-release components, e.g. bicycle wheels. |  |
| Maintenance | A couple of hours' work on general cleaning and maintenance each month; oil to lubricate the chain; occasional tyre change or replacement part. Average cost around £5 a month (£60 a year). | - Service labour costs: £320 pa*<br>- Replacement parts (brake materials, oils, filters, bulbs, wipers, and hoses): £165 pa*<br>- Tyres (based on estimated tyre life of 27,000 miles): £52 pa* |
| Fuel |  | As a rough guide, 10,000 miles a year @ 8.82 pence a mile (based on petrol @ 86.6p/litre) = £882 a year* |
| Road tax |  | £120 a year |
| Breakdown cover |  | £45 a year |
| Other (e.g. tolls, fines, parking, etc.) |  | £180 a year* |

(* Based on annual mileage of 10,000. These costs don't take into account the initial purchase cost or depreciation. Car running and maintenance costs are based on the AA's Running Costs for Petrol Cars, 2008.)

## Travelling abroad

There are many savings to be made when travelling abroad. Ask at your Student Travel Office and compare prices of budget airlines. For travel insurance, use the companies that specialise in insurance for students (page 154). You can claim a **Travel Grant** from the government if you are studying abroad as part of your course for at least a term in the academic year. It is means-tested and the maximum you can receive is equal to the amount you reasonably have to pay, minus the first £303.

## ● Study costs

These include the books you need for your course, stationery, special course materials and equipment, library and photocopying charges, and the costs of any field trips and other events you must attend as part of your study programme.

Before you rush out and buy all the books on your book list, check which ones are essential. If you can't borrow them from the library (and don't forget short-term loan books), try buying copies through a second-hand source such as Amazon Market Place (www.amazon.co.uk) or AbeBooks (www.abebooks.co.uk), or at a local second-hand book store specialising in text books. You may also find course books advertised on university noticeboards – final year students often sell books to raise money before they leave university. Try the Students' Union for stationery.

## ● Phone and Internet

Most students nowadays rely on mobile phones rather than a landline. Broadband is usually included in the rent for university halls of residence, but check to make sure. In the private sector, shared house rents rarely include the cost of the Internet and you will need to share the monthly bill (around £20) with your housemates. There are usually free Internet connections provided in university libraries or elsewhere on campus which can always serve as a back up if you can't get Internet access at your accommodation.

### PHONE BILL TIPS

- Mobile phone users often have to pay more to telephone 'freephone' (08) numbers. Log on to www.saynoto0870.com to find an alternative (cheaper) local number.
- Phone at off-peak times.
- Look for special deals for free evening and weekend calls, and low-cost international calls.
- Avoid unnecessary or costly phone calls.

## Insurance

There are several types of insurance available for students.

Contents and possessions insurance is a must for the many students who bring high value goods and equipment to university (laptops, DVD players, cameras, iPods, sports equipment, bikes, and so on). Contents insurance may also cover damage to your landlord's property and will bring you peace of mind if you are renting private accommodation. If you travel abroad, medical and travel insurance are very important.

### INSURANCE TIP

Before taking out contents and possessions insurance, first ask your parents if you can be included on their household policy.

### Contents and possessions insurance

For students staying in university halls of residence, basic contents and possessions insurance cover may already be included in the rent. This may cover against theft, fire, flood and burst pipes for things in your room such as desktops and laptops, sports equipment and musical instruments, visual and audio equipment (TV, CDs, DVD players), up to a certain value. Endsleigh Student Insurance has teamed up with many halls of residence to provide this cover and you can check on their website whether your hall of residence is part of the scheme (www.endsleigh.co.uk). On the same website you'll find the relevant Certificate of Insurance and details of how to make a claim. If you want to extend the basic cover to include things you take outside your room, and items such as mobile phones and bikes, and to include accidental damage, then you can do this through the Endsleigh website.

For those of you who don't have insurance cover included in your rent, there are several policies to choose from aimed at students living in halls of residence or private rented accommodation. These provide cover at your term time address with options to extend the cover to your parents' home, to temporary accommodation or abroad, and whilst in transit to and from university at the beginning and end of each term. Items are generally covered on a 'new-for-old' basis against loss or damage and theft, except clothing and linen where a deduction is often made for 'wear and tear'. A typical annual premium is between £70 and £280, depending on whether the policy is 'basic' or 'comprehensive' (the latter including extras such as personal accident cover, credit/debit card loss, accidental damage, and cover during vacations). The premium level depends on the value of the items insured, and whether bikes, mobile phones and laptops are included (these often incur additional premiums on top of the standard rates). There are other options such as insurance to cover course fees and rental protection in case you are unable to complete your course for whatever reason. Compare different student policies to find the best deals, such as those at www.cover4students.com and www.endsleigh.co.uk.

## Medical health insurance

Under the NHS, British residents are eligible for free medical care and treatment, but most must pay for prescribed medicines at a subsidised rate. Dental treatment is subsidised by the NHS but there is usually a contribution to make towards the cost of your treatment.

•    International students who intend to stay in the UK for more than six months may register for NHS care (emergency medical treatment is available to everyone without conditions and free of charge). Alternatively, you can take out student health insurance to cover the cost of private medical care at certain surgeries in the UK. In this case, you would pay for your medical treatment and then reclaim the money from your health insurance company. Endsleigh has a travel/health insurance policy for international students studying in the UK for up to a year (www.endsleigh.co.uk).

•    UK students studying abroad must be covered by adequate medical insurance, which should include cover for treatment abroad (as an in-patient or out-patient), costs of returning home should you become seriously ill or disabled, and costs incurred if you die in a foreign country. Some institutions require that you join their medical health insurance scheme – check with the university where you will be studying. Students visiting EU countries should have a valid European Health Insurance card. Endsleigh has a Studying Abroad policy for periods up to 12 months, which includes holidays and trips within a chosen area, as well as hospital care and emergency dental treatment. You may be able to get help from the UK government to cover the costs of medical insurance while studying abroad – check with your student finance provider.

## Travel insurance

There are plenty of different travel insurance policies aimed specifically at students. For example, Endsleigh (www.endsleigh. co.uk) provides a Backpacker policy. This covers loss, damage or theft of baggage (including items such as iPods, MP3 players and cameras, up to a specific value), emergency medical expenses if you are injured during your trip, personal liability legal costs if you cause the injury or death of someone else, and reimbursement for irrecoverable costs after cancellation of the trip due to certain unavoidable circumstances. Cover for a year's backpacking around the world would cost in the region of £300–400, the higher amount if you want cover for such things as delayed or missed departure, loss of personal money and personal accident insurance. Other types of student travel insurance include wintersports insurance, activity insurance and gap year insurance.

## ● Socialising

While there's plenty of hard work at university, it's also crucial that you take time out. Developing a network of friends is not only enjoyable but also improves your overall

### PARTY SPENDING FACTS

In a recent suvey, students were found to spend on average £45 per week on drinks, clubs, pubs, cinema, gigs and parties. The biggest party-goers in terms of money spent were students in Belfast (£55 a week) followed by Leeds and Brighton (around £50). A good third of students say they would rather spend more money on socialising than on a better roof over their heads!

well-being. Share notes and discuss lectures with friends studying the same course, and they may well come to your support if and when you encounter problems. If you are working hard in a part-time job, or living at home, it's worth making the effort to get involved in activities and clubs. Many long-lasting friendships, even life-long partnerships, are made at university.

## Socialising on a shoestring

When it comes to your social life, it's easy for a carefully planned budget to go straight out the window. But there are plenty of ways to have a good time without breaking the bank.

**NIGHT OUT TIPS**

- Take advantage of special deals for students at restaurants, bars and clubs – remember to take along an ID card.
- Go to restaurants where you can take your own drinks.
- Stay within your budget by taking just the cash you can afford and leave your credit card behind.
- Tell your friends not to lend you any money.
- Get to know the owners of a friendly bar or restaurant and you might be in for some perks.
- Go to student events – they are usually subsidised.

If you really are flat broke, then get some friends together to share an evening in – they may well be in the same position as you.

**Student Talk**

*'There are plenty of free ways to socialise, like inviting friends round for a DVD night, with a couple of pizzas in the oven, or playing cards.'*

### Student Talk

'I spend around £20–30 each week socialising. I would recommend getting an NUS card at the beginning of the academic year even though it costs £10. It will save you lots of money on entry fees into clubs, cinema tickets, eating out and clothes shops. I would also recommend attending university/student nights as often the entry is slightly cheaper and the drinks are a lot cheaper.'

'Use Facebook. Often by clicking on 'attending' for events you can be put on a guest list for cheap entry. If you like to drink, consider meeting at someone's house and having a drink before you go out to save on extortionate pub/club prices.'

'Don't take your bank card out with you. Just take out a set amount of money and stick to it. It's so easy if you've got your bank card to think that another £10 won't matter.'

'To be frank, I am so busy studying that I don't go out as much as I should! When I do, it is a lot cheaper at university because of transport. We always arrive for £1 drinks and this saves a great deal of money. University societies run socials, and the ticket often includes a drink or an entrance fee to a club. A night out probably costs me in the region of £10. Very good value!'

# ● Other costs

Finally, there are all the other living costs which gradually use up your Student Loan. For example, sports charges, laundry bills, haircuts, DVDs and CDs, clothes, holidays, TV licence, etc. In a recent survey, student spending on clothes was relatively high: around £20 a week on average, and London students spent the most of all with an average of more than £25.

There are several ways to save on these costs without sacrificing a great deal. For example, you could do without a TV, swap your DVDs and CDs with friends, pose as a model for a free hair cut, camp for a cheap holiday, exercise in the park instead of the gym, buy clothes from vintage and charity shops, even (though not for the faint-hearted) wash your clothes by hand.

## 16 The banks and students

You will need a bank account when you apply for student finance – your loan money and any grants or bursaries will be paid directly into the account. A bank may also offer support and a safety net in times of trouble. Banks welcome students as future potential high earners and there is strong competition between them to attract your custom. This is largely in the form of offers of interest- and fee-free extended overdrafts, and incentives such as cash handouts, discounts on selected items, free cinema tickets, travel insurance or a five-year railcard. The offers differ slightly from bank to bank so do your research. The most important features to look out for are the interest-free overdraft – the amount you can have and for how long – and the rate of interest charged on authorised and unauthorised overdrafts.

Compare student bank accounts at www.moneyfacts. co.uk/money, or check what's on offer by visiting local branches and asking to speak to the student advisor.

## Student Talk

'Internet banking is vital because it's so important to check your bank account regularly – you'll be surprised how quickly little expenditures add up. If you're in trouble, don't put your head in the sand. Cut back on spending and go and see a student advisor if it's serious.'

'Check your finances at least once a week. I had a problem with fraudulent use of my account and didn't notice for a month – fraud does happen, even to people without any money!'

'I recommend setting up an online account because you can check your finances from home or even get your parents to keep an eye on you if you are an extreme spender!'

'Have two accounts so that you can put your rent money into one and forget about it. It pretty much guarantees being able to pay your rent. Then you can just divide what is left by 10 to cover all the weeks of term.'

'Don't open many bank accounts that have overdrafts as if they are available you are more likely to use them.'

'It was very easy even for an international student like me to open an account. I use Internet banking and keep a regular eye on my USA bills.'

**BANKING TIPS**

- When choosing an account, look behind the perks. The interest-free overdraft is the most valuable benefit (it can be a saviour when you're waiting for your next loan payment to clear). Check the interest-free amounts. Most accounts offer increasing amounts as the years go on. Some offer large amounts from day one. Other incentives offered by the banks are useful if they save you money: a free railcard is good if you use the trains; travel insurance is worthless if you can't afford to go anywhere. Check also how long you can keep using the same account after graduation, and whether there is then an option to open a graduate account with preferential rates.

- Locate the branch of your chosen bank closest to your university and find out if there is a student advisor there who you can go and see if you encounter problems.

- Bank online to keep a close check on your account. It saves paper and postage too.

- When your Student Loan money arrives in your current account, transfer the bulk of it to a savings account where it may earn a little interest, and then each week or month transfer the amount you need to live on back to the current account.

- Be careful about borrowing on your overdraft – you'll have to pay it back eventually.

- Never borrow over your overdraft limit without asking the bank first and agreeing an authorised limit. Bank charges can roll in at £15 or more, up to £20 per day for unauthorised borrowing. Clocking up just £100 over your limit can lead to fees higher than this within the space of a week. If you do exceed your limit, go immediately in person to your branch to talk to your student finance advisor who may suggest a helpful solution.

- Don't be afraid to speak to your student finance advisor if you get into unexpected debt, and the sooner the better.

## 17  Managing your money

Going to university may be the first time you are completely responsible for your own finances. Drawing up a budget to check that you have sufficient income in terms of loans, grants and bursaries to cover all your costs is essential before you go out spending. Above all, remember to keep a check on your finances so that money worries do not detract from your studies and from enjoying university life.

Here are four steps to managing your money:

- **Step 1: Work out a budget**

We recommend that you work out an annual budget, to include vacations, and from this you can calculate how much you will have to spend each week. There is an example of an annual budget on page 167. First calculate all your likely expenditure (everything you will pay for) while you are studying, including 'hidden' costs such as laundry and library charges, unexpected bills (a college ball or a study tour), as well as the larger items – tuition fees, rent, food and books, etc. Your expected costs of studying will then give you an idea of how much you will need to

> **BUDGET TIP**
>
> It is strongly recommended that you draw up a budget before you begin your course and keep control of your money right from the start.

borrow from the government, for example in Student Loans, and from other sources.

- **Step 2: Balance the books**

If the funds available from the public purse are not enough to cover your expected expenditure, think about what other sources of income you may have (for example, savings from a gap year, a generous gift from a relative…). If your expected outgoings still exceed your incomings, think about how you might reduce your expenditure. For example, by making savings on meals out, new clothes and public transport. Also consider getting a part-time job (like nearly half the UK student population), and vacation work if necessary.

- **Step 3: Stick to your budget**

Once you have juggled the figures and have a budget that balances (more or less), then all you need to do is stick to it. This will be easier if your budget is realistic, i.e. the figures accurately reflect your particular case. Student budgets tend to be very tight and you may find it difficult not to overspend. If your debts get out of hand, and your family cannot help, you can apply for Hardship Funds (page 52). Get advice from your Student Services department or the student advisor at your bank, who may be able to arrange an extension to your overdraft. Other sources of help include your local Citizens Advice Bureau (check the phone book) or a debt advice agency such as National Debtline (www.nationaldebtline.co.uk, telephone 0808 808 4000).

**➤ SHORTFALL IN FUNDS!**
A recent NUS survey estimates an average shortfall in funds of £7,408 per academic year for students in London and £6,683 for students elsewhere, after taking into account what they are likely to receive from Student Loans, Grants and bursaries.
(Source: NUS 2007/08)

- ### Step 4: Adjusting your budget

You may need to adjust your budget in your second year if you find that your expenditure estimates were not accurate or if your income level changes.

**BUDGET SHEET TO DOWNLOAD**
You can download a free budget sheet at The Complete University Guide (www.thecompleteuniversityguide.co.uk) under the section 'Managing your Money, Budgeting'.

---

### Student Talk

'Try writing down every penny you spend in a week to see where it's going and how much you spend, then cut £5 (or more!) off that figure and get that amount of cash out for the coming week. By paying in cash you know how much you're spending.'

'I do keep a regular check but my money just disappears because it's so easy to spend money while I'm here.'

'Before coming to university, my parents gave me a spending plan on Microsoft Excel, which basically has a list of all the things I spend money on at university, i.e. drinks, taxis, food, and it adds up what I've spent each week and takes it off my weekly budget, so I know where I stand and how much money I have left for the week.'

## Student Talk

'At the beginning of the week I take out a week's worth of cash (£50), buy my weekly shopping, then what's left is mine for the week. If I don't spend it all I put it in a jar to use if I run out another week.'

'Go back through your accounts at the end of the first term. This will help you work out how to budget for the rest of the year (i.e. how much you actually do spend!).'

'I try not to look at my expenditure because it makes me panic. I spend so much money and can never stick to a budget.'

'I would recommend not to take cash out every day or when needed. It is more effective to take cash out at the beginning of the week then use this as your budget.'

'If you know there's something you want to buy that's going to need a large proportion of your weekly allowance, have a cheaper week with fewer nights out. Watch a film instead!'

'Try to budget from day one. It may seem like a lot of money but believe me it swiftly goes. I got into the horrible habit of not checking because I knew it would be bad news!'

'I do a spreadsheet, and every week put in my expenditure. It takes a bit of time, but is good so that I can budget for things like Christmas.'

## Your annual budget: a practical example

Budgeting accurately is never an easy process, and we have constructed this simple but realistic annual income and expenditure summary to make monitoring and controlling your finances easier. This is a budget for non-smokers and assumes the latest findings of an average weekly spend of £40 on food (eating in and out) and £45 on socialising. For the quarter of you who smoke, an additional outlay of around £20 may be needed – is it worth it? Don't be too optimistic in your first budget, and do be aware of how much you actually spend (try writing down everything you spend over a week or so). Budget for university gigs and balls, birthdays and parties, or you may find yourself missing out on the best social events of the year.

You'll need to list all your income and all your expenditure as in the table on page 167.

1.    In the column marked 'Expenditure' write down all the costs you are likely to incur over the year: tuition fees, rent, utility bills, food, travel, phone, socialising, study materials, insurance, library charges, clothes, laundry bills, etc. It can be difficult to predict accurately some variable expenses, such as socialising. Start by identifying bills which must be paid – use the examples in this book as an estimate of typical costs. Then make sure you include a contingency for emergencies. This will leave you with the 'flexible' part of your income to cover your other spending.

If you plan to support yourself during term time and to stay at home in the holidays, then multiply any weekly spending by the number of weeks you'll be away from home. This would be approximately 30 weeks for a standard undergraduate course. However, many students spend time away from home during the

**INCOME TIP**

When drawing up an annual budget, remember that the income you receive in Student Loans, Grants, bursaries, etc, has to last you through the holidays to the beginning of the next term.

vacations, so you may need to support yourself for longer than 30 weeks a year – a good average is 39 weeks. Even if you do spend all of your vacations at home, you should allow for the occasional drink with friends, etc. Now add up the expenditure column.

2.    In the column headed 'Income', list your likely income over the year from the various public and private sources, for example a Student Loan, Grant, bursary or scholarship, your parents' contribution if any, and money from savings, employment, etc. Then add up the income figures.

3.    Subtract the total expenditure from the total income to find your budget surplus or shortfall. If there is a big gap between planned expenditure and expected income, perhaps your spending habits need attention and you may need to consider increasing your income by working during the vacations and/or term time. If you are fortunate enough to have a budget surplus, you can plan to put some money away in a savings account in case of unexpected bills later on, or use it to pay off your Student Loan more quickly when you start earning.

4.    Once you have drawn up your annual budget, give yourself weekly limits on spending by dividing the annual sums by the number of weeks during which you have to support yourself. In the example below you would have around £40 per week to spend in the supermarket and on eating out. This is a figure you can check on a weekly basis – make sure you don't spend more than this!

## AN ANNUAL STUDENT BUDGET

| INCOME (annual) | £ | EXPENDITURE (annual) | £ |
|---|---|---|---|
| Tuition Fee Loan | 3,225 | Tuition fee | 3,225 |
| Maintenance Loan | 3,497 | Rent | 3,200 |
| Parental contribution | - | Utility bills | Included in rent |
| Maintenance Grant/ Special Support Grant | 2,906 | Food (eating in and out) | 1,550 |
| Bursary or Scholarship | 319 | Travel using public transport during term time and to and from home plus the occasional taxi ride | 900 |
| Any additional grants or allowances | 0 | Study costs, including books, course materials, photocopying, library costs, etc | 500 |
| Savings | 400 | Mobile phone and Internet | 200 (for mobile – broadband is included in rent) |
| Earnings from part-time work during term time | 2,700 | Insurance | 100 (for an upgrade to the basic cover included in rent) |
| Earnings during vacations | 500 | Socialising | 1,750 |
| Bank overdraft | 0 | Toiletries | 250 |
| | | Laundry | 150 |
| | | Clothes and shoes | 450 |
| | | Home entertainment (DVDs, CDs, etc) and presents | 300 |
| | | Sports and leisure | 200 |
| | | Costs during the vacations | 500 |
| | | Emergencies | 500 |
| TOTAL INCOME | 13,547 | TOTAL EXPENDITURE | 13,775 |
| (Shortfall) | | | (-228) |

## Note:

In this example, we have assumed that you live in England and have decided to go to university in another part of England (other than London) so you will not be living at home. You have decided to take out a Tuition Fee Loan to cover the full tuition fee of £3,225, you are in receipt of the maximum Maintenance Loan plus Grant of £6,403 (because your household income is £25,000) and the university has given you a minimum standard bursary of £319. Your accommodation is a place in a university halls of residence, with shared bathroom and self-catering facilities (around £80 a week for 39 weeks, including electricity, gas, water, broadband Internet and basic insurance cover for contents and possessions). For an ensuite room you can expect to pay over £4,000 per year.

The shortfall of £228 is in addition to the two loans from the Student Loans Company (the Tuition Fee Loan and the Maintenance Loan) which will be carried forward as a debt to be repaid after you graduate.

*Committed to sustainability, the University of Gloucestershire was the first English university to satisfy the requirements of the environmental standard ISO 14001. It has solar power, green electricity and a bicycle loan scheme.*

## 18   Survival tips for students on a budget

Surviving on a student budget can be challenging. Here are our final top tips for making your money stretch that bit further.

- Plan ahead, be organised and learn how to budget – before you begin your course, work out how much money you can spend each week and what you will spend it on, and stick to it.
- Sign on with the bank which offers the best long-term benefits, including an interest-free overdraft.
- Don't be tempted by the loan sharks that charge extortionate rates of interest to people who can least afford it, or to borrow on a credit card when you know you won't be able to pay it off by the date given on your statement – the interest rates are also very high. Only borrow money from the Student Loans scheme or recognised student sources of finance such as banks (including your family!).
- Find a part-time job and arrange to be paid gross if you are not liable for tax.
- Go online to find the best discounts, and make the most of student offers.
- Avoid excessive spending during freshers' week.
- Set yourself a weekly cash budget rather than taking a credit card or cheque book with you when you go shopping.
- Get to know how to use the library at the earliest opportunity.

- Find out which books you really need on your book list before buying.
- Buy second-hand books. Textbooks in good condition can be bought for half price through the Amazon website (www.amazon.co.uk), or try a second-hand book store specialising in course books. Look out for book sales on campus.
- Learn to cook and invite friends over rather than going out.
- Swap DVDs, music, books, clothes.
- Shop in local markets, charity shops and the Students' Union.
- Go green and save on household bills.
- Buy products in the value ranges at supermarkets.
- Save on public transport (and save the planet) by walking or investing in a bike.
- If you don't need something, do without. Plenty of students survive without their own TV (students still have to pay over £100 for a TV licence). Don't be tempted by 'two for the price of one' offers when you don't want one in the first place.
- Collect your loose change in a jar. It may come in handy.

**Student Talk**

'Remember how much you're paying for your studying and try to achieve a balance of studying and socialising.'

'Stick to a budget because you don't want to be skint at the end of term when you should be celebrating! There's nothing more annoying than wanting to go out with your friends in the last week of term, only to find that no one can afford it.'

'Know how much money you have got and the essentials you need to buy, so you don't end up spending all your money on socialising and have none left to buy a toilet roll.'

'Before you buy anything, ask yourself – do I need this?'

'Talk to people! Loads of students have money issues at university so talk to other people or ask your personal tutor. Universities have welfare systems to help people having financial troubles.'

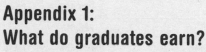

# Appendix 1:
# What do graduates earn?

The table overleaf shows graduate earnings in their first jobs across a range of subjects. The earnings are significantly higher for graduates in graduate jobs than for graduates in non-graduate employment. Note that the figures do not reflect your earning prospects as your career develops!

## GRADUATE EARNINGS

| Subject | Graduate Employment or Self-Employment | Non-Graduate Employment or Self-Employment |
| --- | --- | --- |
| Medicine | £28,897 | |
| Dentistry | £28,813 | |
| Chemical Engineering | £26,366 | £16,553 |
| Economics | £25,101 | £17,316 |
| Veterinary Medicine | £24,762 | |
| General Engineering | £23,876 | £15,349 |
| Mechanical Engineering | £23,572 | £17,426 |
| Middle Eastern & African Studies | £23,414 | £17,692 |
| Civil Engineering | £23,387 | £15,444 |
| Social Work | £23,328 | £15,572 |
| Aeronautical & Manufacturing Engineering | £22,965 | £16,482 |
| Building | £22,941 | £19,484 |
| Land & Property Management | £22,883 | |
| Mathematics | £22,882 | £16,136 |
| Electrical & Electronic Engineering | £22,543 | £16,585 |
| Physics & Astronomy | £22,247 | £16,234 |
| Russian | £21,835 | £17,202 |
| Computer Science | £21,714 | £16,370 |
| Philosophy | £21,466 | £15,312 |
| Geology | £21,400 | £15,563 |
| Business Studies | £21,071 | £16,161 |
| Nursing | £20,967 | £15,434 |
| Politics | £20,877 | £15,364 |
| Accounting & Finance | £20,586 | £16,614 |
| Iberian Languages | £20,473 | £15,865 |

## GRADUATE EARNINGS

| | | |
|---|---|---|
| French | £20,425 | £16,012 |
| Town & Country Planning and Landscape | £20,268 | £17,133 |
| Italian | £20,201 | £16,636 |
| Education | £20,116 | £13,781 |
| German | £19,971 | £15,364 |
| Librarianship & Information Management | £19,958 | £15,904 |
| East & South Asian Studies | £19,821 | £16,316 |
| Law | £19,805 | £15,693 |
| Chemistry | £19,799 | £15,121 |
| Food Science | £19,710 | £15,245 |
| Social Policy | £19,550 | £14,079 |
| Geography & Environmental Sciences | £19,545 | £14,800 |
| Anthropology | £19,485 | £15,619 |
| Classics & Ancient History | £19,422 | £16,078 |
| Other Subjects Allied to Medicine | £19,418 | £14,750 |
| History | £19,198 | £14,636 |
| Theology & Religious Studies | £19,141 | £14,424 |
| Anatomy & Physiology | £19,008 | £15,400 |
| History of Art, Architecture and Design | £18,975 | £15,749 |
| Pharmacology & Pharmacy | £18,944 | £14,422 |
| Materials Technology | £18,871 | £14,764 |
| American Studies | £18,757 | £14,534 |
| Biological Sciences | £18,687 | £13,914 |
| Architecture | £18,626 | £15,357 |
| Hospitality, Leisure, Recreation & Tourism | £18,602 | £15,222 |
| Sports Science | £18,562 | £14,156 |
| English | £18,484 | £14,263 |
| Agriculture & Forestry | £18,333 | £15,047 |

## GRADUATE EARNINGS

| | | |
|---|---|---|
| Sociology | £18,293 | £14,528 |
| Psychology | £18,091 | £13,999 |
| Linguistics | £17,681 | £14,535 |
| Communication & Media Studies | £17,549 | £14,484 |
| Art & Design | £17,327 | £14,086 |
| Drama, Dance & Cinematics | £17,260 | £14,340 |
| Archaeology | £17,065 | £14,473 |
| Music | £17,017 | £14,217 |
| Celtic Studies | £16,604 | £16,524 |
| Total | £20,763 | £15,009 |

Mean salaries of full-time, first degree leavers entering employment or self-employment. Source: HESA 2006/07. Check www.thecompleteuniversity guide.co.uk for updated figures.

# Appendix 2:
# Bursaries and scholarships
# 2009/10: additional information

This appendix is intended to supplement the information provided in the tables on pages 32–47. Check the current 'University Profiles' on www.thecompleteuniversityguide. co.uk for updates.

## University of Aberdeen
• Tuition fees for non-Scottish domiciled students for 2009/10: £1,820 pa (£2,895 for Medicine). If you are a Scottish-domiciled first degree student you are eligible for your tuition fees to be covered by the Scottish government. Scottish students should apply to the SAAS to cover this cost. Students from England, Wales and Northern Ireland should apply for a Tuition Fee Loan to Student Finance England, Student Finance Wales, and Student Finance Northern Ireland as appropriate. Students from elsewhere in the EU should contact the SAAS.
• The RUK bursary has been introduced for students normally resident in England, Wales or Northern Ireland only, studying at a Scottish university, who would otherwise have been eligible for a £319 national minimum bursary (i.e. in receipt of full Maintenance Grant) had they studied at a university in the rest of the UK. The RUK bursary is currently worth around £310.
• Fees for placement year and year abroad are normally 50 per cent of full-time fee.
• For more information: www.abdn.ac.uk

## University of Abertay Dundee
• Tuition fees for non-Scottish domiciled students for 2009/10: £1,820 pa (£2,895 for Medicine). If you are a Scottish-domiciled first degree student you are eligible for your tuition fees to be covered by the Scottish government. Scottish students should apply to the SAAS to cover this cost. Students from England, Wales and Northern Ireland should apply for a Tuition Fee Loan to Student Finance England, Student Finance Wales, and Student Finance Northern Ireland as appropriate. Students from elsewhere in the EU should contact the SAAS.
• The RUK bursary has been introduced for students normally resident in England, Wales or Northern Ireland only, studying at a Scottish university, who would otherwise have been eligible for a £319 national minimum bursary (i.e. in receipt of full Maintenance Grant) had they studied at a university in the rest of the UK. The RUK bursary is currently worth around £310.
• Fees for placement year and year abroad are normally 50 per cent of full-time fee.
• For more information: www.abertay.ac.uk

## Aberystwyth University
• Tuition fees (2009): £3,225.
• Placement year/year abroad tuition fee: £625 (2008/09). No fee for full industrial year.
• Students from Wales will be eligible for a non means-tested Fee Grant (£1,940) from the Welsh Assembly Government towards the cost of tuition fees.

- All bursaries and scholarships are open to full-time UK and EU undergraduate students and are paid in instalments each term. The value shown is the total amount payable for each award.
- Entrance scholarships: £3,000–£3,600 plus an unconditional offer and the option of residing in university accommodation throughout the course. Awarded on the basis of exam performance.
- Excellence bursaries in specified subjects: £2,000 for students who achieve 300 UCAS points and enrol on courses in Science, European Languages, Welsh and defined Welsh-medium schemes.
- Residential bursaries: £500 in the form of a reduction of hall fees for students in their first year.
- Sports bursaries (£1,500), music bursaries (£1,200), bursary for care leavers (£3,000–£5,400)
- Eligible students must apply through UCAS by 30 June (15 January for Entrance scholarships) and make Aberystwyth first choice by the UCAS deadline.
- For more information: www.aber.ac.uk

## Anglia Ruskin University
- In receipt of full Maintenance Grant: £319.
- Tuition fees (2009): £3,225.
- Tuition fee for placement year and year abroad will be half the prevailing tuition fee.
- Non repayable, non means-tested scholarship to UK and EU undergraduate students who pay the full tuition fee. Worth £500 for each year of course.
- 12 Foundation Scholarships worth up to £750 are offered each year to students studying at Anglia Ruskin University to assist with a period outside the UK to undertake a study visit in connection with their chosen course.
- Awards range from £500 to £1,000 per year, with payments split by semester, and are available in a variety of sports including cricket, rowing, athletics and swimming. Conditions apply.
- For more information: www.anglia.ac.uk

## Arts University College Bournemouth
- In receipt of full Maintenance Grant: £350.
- In receipt of partial Maintenance Grant: £200.
- Tuition fees (2009): £3,225.
- Students will also receive a bonus of £150 on successful completion of their first year, £250 after their second year and a further £500 upon completion of their final year.
- All students who receive a grant of £1,075 – £2,905, will receive a sum of £200.

- Up to 30 students from designated target groups will receive a 25 per cent reduction on halls fees.
- All students from designated schools and colleges will receive up to £350 per year for bus company travel cards.
- Students who receive a grant of £1,075 or above will receive up to £175 in vouchers for bicycles and accessories.
- Students from care will receive an additional £2,000 per year.
- For more information: www.aib.ac.uk

## Aston University
- Household income below £18,000: £800 min.
- Household incomes between £18–38,000: £0–640.
- Tuition fees (2009): £3,225.
- Tuition fee for placement year and year abroad: £1,610. However, placement bursaries of £1,000 are available to all Aston students on their placement year and allowances and awards worth a total of £1,500 are available to all Aston students on their year abroad or during unpaid placement years. (Around 95 per cent of placements are paid – average £14,000. 70 per cent of Aston University students take placement year/sandwich programmes or a year abroad.)
- For more information: www.aston.ac.uk

## Bangor University
- In receipt of full or partial Maintenance Grant: £1,000–£500.
- Living in region scholarship.
- Sport scholarship.
- Academic achievement scholarship.
- Subject bursary.
- Tuition fees (2009): £3,225.
- Fees for placement year and year abroad (except Erasmus) 2008: £625.
- Students from Wales will be eligible for a non means-tested Fee Grant (£1,890) from the Welsh Assembly government towards the cost of tuition fees.
- The Bangor Bursary Scheme aims to provide additional support for those from lower income families. Depending on household income this could be £1,000 or £500 a year for students on full-time undergraduate courses at Bangor University.
- Start-up bursaries for those entering university from care worth £1,000.
- As part of the university's drive to support and develop a number of subject areas of regional or national importance, Bangor will be offering subject-specific bursary awards of £500 for those studying courses within the following Academic Schools for 2009 entry:

Chemistry, Computer Science, Electronic Engineering, Law and Modern Languages.
• About 40 merit scholarships worth up to £3,000 for excellence in the annual entrance scholarships examinations.
• Excellence scholarships of £5,000 may be available in specific subject areas. These scholarships, which are non means-tested and payable in the first year only, will be awarded to the UK/EU students coming to Bangor with the highest academic attainment in the relevant subject areas.
• For more information: www.bangor.ac.uk

## University of Bath
• In receipt of full Maintenance Grant: £1,200.
• In receipt of partial Maintenance Grant: £300–£900.
• Living in region sport scholarship.
• Academic achievement scholarship.
• Subject bursary.
• Tuition fees (2009): £3,225.
• Merit scholarships of £1,000.
• Engineering scholarships for those living in the region with exceptional ability.
• Choral scholarships.
• Sports scholarships.
• A small number of merit-based fees scholarships for international students.
• For more information: www.bath.ac.uk

## Bath Spa University
• In receipt of full Maintenance Grant: £1,200–£350.
• In receipt of partial Maintenance Grant: £200–£100.
• Tuition fees (2009): £3,225.
• Fees for placement year expected to be £1,610. Fees for full year abroad: no fee. Fees for part year abroad: £3,225.
• Scholarships worth £1,000 in named single honours science-based subjects will not be means-tested.
• 30 per cent of the additional fee income will be used to assist students from low-income families.
• For more information: www.bathspa.ac.uk

## University of Bedfordshire
• In receipt of full Maintenance Grant (2008): £820.
• In receipt of partial Maintenance Grant (2008): £310–£615.
• Academic achievement scholarship.

- Tuition fees (2009): £3,225.
- Tuition fee for Foundation degree is £1,285 for home/EU students. Tuition fees for 'sandwich year-out' home/EU students is £1,615. (Full cost fees apply to non-EU students and 'second degree' students.)
- 40 per cent of additional fee income to be earmarked for bursaries.
- For more information: www.beds.ac.uk

## Birkbeck
- The Birkbeck Student Opportunity Fund offers a limited number of non-repayable bursaries of £1,500 a year for the full four years of a first degree. These support students in financial need, who are ineligible for government-funded fee and course grants.
- For more information: www.bbk.ac.uk

## University of Birmingham
- In receipt of full Maintenance: Grant £860.
- In receipt of partial Maintenance Grant: £860.
- Shortage subjects scholarship.
- Academic achievement scholarship: £1,290.
- Tuition fees (2009): £3,225.
- Tuition fee for placement year and year abroad (2009): £1,615. (NB: Students who are liable to pay half the tuition fee on their year abroad, i.e. not Erasmus students, will receive a travel grant of £300.)
- Scholarships are available to students who meet the criteria for the award of a Birmingham Grant and, in addition, obtain A levels of AAB or better, or 34 or more points in the International Baccalaureate, or DDD in BTec (other qualifications considered on a case by case basis).
- Part-time employment, paid volunteering and placement opportunities will be created by the university as supplementary income sources.
- Payment will be made in two instalments.
- For more information: www.as.bham.ac.uk

## Birmingham City University
- In receipt of full Maintenance Grant: up to £525 available in 2008/09.
- In receipt of partial Maintenance Grant: up to £525 available in 2008/09.
- Tuition fees (2009): £3,225.
- Placement year tuition fees (2008): £750.
- Eleven per cent of additional fee income to be earmarked for bursaries.
- For more information: www.bcu.ac.uk

## Bishop Grosseteste University College

- In receipt of full Maintenance Grant: £1,075.
- In receipt of partial Maintenance Grant: £1,075.
- Tuition fees (2009): £3,225.
- Care Leavers' Bursary of £3,600 for 2009/10.
- For more information: www.bishopg.ac.uk

## University of Bolton

- Tuition fees (2009): £3,225.
- The Bolton Bursary: the university is providing bursaries to students in receipt of a full or partial Maintenance Grant. The full bursary for eligible students is £350 per year. It is non-repayable.
- Bolton Scholarship: £750 will be paid to the student over the academic year irrespective of the family's financial means. Terms and conditions apply; for the criteria for this scholarship please visit the website.
- Excellence scholarship: £500 per annum will be awarded to all full-time UK undergraduate students, irrespective of their financial means, who progress to a university undergraduate higher education course having successfully accumulated a minimum of 300 UCAS points at A2 Level or equivalent.
- Care Leavers' Scholarship: £1,000 per annum will be awarded to full-time UK undergraduate students leaving a care background, irrespective of their financial means, who progress to a university undergraduate higher education course.
- Vice-Chancellor's award: a one off payment of £15,000 paid over the duration of the course will be awarded to the most outstanding academically-gifted full-time UK undergraduate students, irrespective of their financial means, who progress to a university undergraduate higher education course. Students in receipt of the Vice Chancellor's award will not be eligible to receive the Bolton, Excellence or Care leavers' scholarships.
- All figures quoted for the 2009/10 awards are subject to confirmation.
- For more information: www.bolton.ac.uk

## Bournemouth University

- In receipt of full Maintenance Grant: £319.
- In receipt of partial Maintenance Grant: up to £319.
- Progressing from outreach bursary: £500.
- Sport scholarship.
- Academic achievement scholarship.
- Tuition fees (2009): £3,225.
- Placement year tuition fee will be around £525.
- Bursary available to Home and EU students (EU students eligible for a maximum of £1,000).

• . Home and EU students studying at most partner institutions are also eligible for a further £500.
• Scholarship scheme to reward academic and vocational merit and success in sport, music and citizenship, worth up to £1,000, made either 'in kind' or in cash.
• Awards made on the basis of family income.
• 27 per cent of additional tuition fee income will be earmarked for bursaries.
• For more information: www.bournemouth.ac.uk

## University of Bradford
• In receipt of full Maintenance Grant:  £500–£900.
• In receipt of partial Maintenance Grant: £400–£600.
• Progressing from outreach scholarship: £300.
• Tuition fees (2009): £3,225.
• Placement year and year abroad tuition fee (2008): £625.
• The University of Bradford bursary is available to all home and EU students who are eligible for receipt of a Higher Education Maintenance Grant. The maximum bursary, payable to students whose family income is below £40,000, is: Foundation year: £500; Year 1: £500; Year 2: £700; Year 3: £900. For students in receipt of a partial Maintenance Grant whose family income is between £40,001 and £60,032 the bursary is £400, £400, £500 and £600 respectively.
• The bursary is paid in one instalment in March.
• For more information: www.brad.ac.uk

## University of Brighton
• In receipt of full Maintenance Grant: £1,080 max.
• In receipt of partial Maintenance Grant: £540 min.
• Disabled bursary.
• Academic achievement scholarship.
• Sport scholarship.
• Tuition fees (2009): £3,225.
• Placement year tuition fee will be £710. Year abroad (excluding Erasmus) tuition fee will be £710.
• Care leaver study grant: £1,000 a year.
• Up to five disabled sports scholarships: £1,000.
• 21 university scholarships of £1,000 to the first and second year students who perform most strongly in their end of year assessments. A small number of additional scholarships will be available for students entering the third year of four-year programmes in 2009/10. Scholarships are for one year only.
• For more information: www.brighton.ac.uk

## University of Bristol

- In receipt of full Maintenance Grant: £1,200.
- In receipt of partial Maintenance Grant: £770–£310 on a sliding scale.
- Living in region bursary.
- Sport scholarship.
- Shortage subjects.
- Academic achievement scholarship.
- Tuition fees (2009): £3,225.
- Placement year and year abroad tuition fee: 50 per cent relevant tuition fee.
- Means-tested local bursary worth £1,075 for students resident in either the BS or BA postal codes at the time of their UCAS application and in receipt of a Maintenance Grant.
- 12 Vice-Chancellor's scholarships valued at £3,000 a year will be awarded to undergraduate students with exceptional musical, dramatic or sporting talent. (The scheme is designed to attract students with exceptional abilities outside their normal field of study.)
- Alumni academic achievement awards valued at up to £1,000 a year will be awarded to the top first year students as identified by each faculty.
- Access to Bristol Bursary valued at £3,225 in 2009 will be awarded to students from particular schools and colleges defined by the Widening Participation and Undergraduate Recruitment Office and who have successfully completed the Access to Bristol scheme.
- 17 per cent of additional fee income (£987,000 in 2006/07) will be earmarked for bursaries.
- For more information: www.bristol.ac.uk

## Brunel University

- In receipt of full Maintenance Grant: £1,000.
- In receipt of partial Maintenance Grant: £500.
- Living in specified postcodes scholarship.
- Progressing from outreach scholarship.
- Ethnic minorities scholarship.
- Academic achievement scholarship.
- Tuition fees (2009): £3,225.
- Placement year tuition fee (2009): £815. Fee levels vary depending on thick or thin sandwich course. Consult the university for full details.
- Up to 25 scholarships worth up to £3,000 for high-performing students from partnership schools in low-participation boroughs. (Terms and conditions apply.)
- For more information: www.brunel.ac.uk

## University of Buckingham
For information: www.buckingham.ac.uk

## Buckinghamshire New University
• In receipt of full Maintenance Grant: £500.
• Tuition fees (2009): £3,225.
• £500 Bucks Bursaries for all students. These bursaries will be universally available and will be promoted widely as part of Bucks' strategy to encourage the widest possible range of applicants.
• £300 Bucks Scholarships. These scholarships will be targeted at new students enrolling at the university from schools and colleges with which Bucks has developed a formal strategic relationship.
• For more information: www.bucks.ac.uk

## University of Cambridge
• In receipt of full Maintenance Grant: £3,250.
• In receipt of partial Maintenance Grant: £50–£2,000.
• Mature students who are Cambridge residents and are recipients of the full Maintenance Grant will be eligible for an enhanced bursary of £5,400.
• Tuition fees (2009): £3,225.
• Year abroad tuition fee will be half the standard tuition fee.
• Students from Scotland, Wales and Northern Ireland may be eligible for bursaries, subject to assessment.
• 30 per cent of additional fee income (£7 million in 2010/11) will be earmarked for bursaries.
• Also financial support for disabled students and students with dependent children.
• For more information: www.cam.ac.uk

## Canterbury Christ Church University
• In receipt of full Maintenance Grant: £860.
• In receipt of partial Maintenance Grant: £535.
• Tuition fees (2009): £3,225.
• Placement year and year abroad tuition fee (2009): £1,610.
• Six sport scholarships valued at £2,000 a year and 7 scholarships of £500 a year.
• Music scholarships valued at £25–£1,500 a year.
• For more information: www.canterbury.ac.uk

## Cardiff University
• In receipt of full Maintenance Grant: £1,050.
• In receipt of partial Maintenance Grant: £500.

- Academic excellence scholarship.
- Tuition fees (2009): £3,225.
- Students from Wales will be eligible for a non means-tested Fee Grant (£1,940) from the Welsh Assembly government towards the cost of tuition fees.
- Placement year/year abroad tuition fee will be 50 per cent (except Erasmus).
- Cardiff University scholarships worth £3,000 for academic excellence in specified subject areas.
- For more information: www.cardiff.ac.uk

## University of Central Lancashire
- Tuition fees (2009): £3,225.
- University bursary 2009 will be £500 per qualifying student in the first year of study, £310 in subsequent years for eligible students, where the principal earner in the household in which the student lives earns less than £60,000 gross per year.
- Excellence sport scholarships of £4,000.
- Gilbertson Scholarship of £3,300 will be available to First Class degree holders progressing to postgraduate study at the university.
- Harris Bursaries are available to students facing hardship (up to a maximum of £1,000 per year).
- For more information: www.uclan.ac.uk

## Central School of Speech and Drama
- In receipt of full Maintenance Grant: £500.
- Tuition fees (2009): £3,225.
- Other endowed bursaries and scholarships may be available.
- For more information: www.cssd.ac.uk

## University of Chester
- In receipt of full Maintenance Grant: £1,000.
- Tuition fees (2009): £3,225.
- Fees for placement year: £1,570.
- For more information: www.chester.ac.uk

## University of Chichester
- In receipt of full Maintenance Grant: £1,077.
- In receipt of partial Maintenance Grant: £0–1,026.
- Tuition fees (2009): £3,225.
- Placement year tuition fee: £1,570.
- For more information: www.chiuni.ac.uk

## City University
- In receipt of full Maintenance Grant: £750.
- In receipt of partial Maintenance Grant: £350.
- Living in specified postcodes scholarship.
- Shortage subjects scholarship.
- Tuition fees (2009): £3,225.
- 15 per cent of additional fee income will be earmarked for bursaries; 2 per cent for scholarships.
- For more information: www.city.ac.uk

## Courtauld Institute of Art
- In receipt of full or partial Maintenance Grant: £319.
- Tuition fees (2009): £3,225.
- Courtauld Bursary. The Institute will also award bursaries of £4,000 to four students in receipt of the full Higher Education Maintenance Grant who come from a group defined by HESA as being under-represented in Higher Education. Priority shall be given to students: i) who have been educated in the state sector (where Art History is not normally offered as part of the curriculum), ii) who live in neighbourhoods defined as having low higher education participation rates, iii) who come from families classified as socio-economic groups 4–7.
- For more information: www.courtauld.ac.uk

## Coventry University
- In receipt of full or partial Maintenance Grant: £320.
- Tuition fees (2009): £3,225.
- Scholarships available for academic excellence, excellence in performance in sport, music, enterprise. Also for continuing students and in shortage subjects. Scholarships are worth around £2,000 and are subject to conditions.
- For more information: www.coventry.ac.uk

## University of Cumbria
- In receipt of full Maintenance Grant: £1,290.
- In receipt of partial Maintenance Grant: £215–£1,070.
- Tuition fees (2009): £3,225.
- 35 scholarships of £1,000. Students should meet defined criteria and be active in one of the following areas: community, sport, creative arts, environment, business enterprise and entrepreneurship.
- For more information: www.cumbria.ac.uk

## De Montfort University
- In receipt of full Maintenance Grant: £500.
- In receipt of partial Maintenance Grant: £500.

- Tuition fees (2009): £3,225.
- Placement year tuition fee (2009): £625 (to be confirmed).
- Year abroad tuition fee (2008): £3,145.
- Regional bursary: £250.
- £1,000 Looked-after Children Bursary for students entering university from care.
- £1,000 academic scholarship for students with at least 280 UCAS tariff points.
- Creative industries scholarships of £2,000 for students with at least 320 UCAS tariff points.
- £1,000 Opportunities scholarship for students with an Access qualification. 200 awards available.
- For more information: www.dmu.ac.uk

## University of Derby
- In receipt of full Maintenance Grant: £830.
- In receipt of partial Maintenance Grant: £210 £520.
- Living in region bursary: £300.
- Living in specified postcode bursary: £300.
- Progressing from outreach bursary: £400.
- You could get up to £1,230 a year from Derby.
- If you're starting in September 2009 and will be paying £2,055 or £3,225 a year course fees you could benefit from either one or both of the following bursaries (if you qualify for more than one of these bursaries, the maximum amount you can get is £400): local bursary of £300 if you live in the DE, NG, LE, B, ST, S, SK, DN, PE, CV or WS postcode areas; bursary of £400 if you join Derby from one of their local Compact partner schools or colleges.
- For home students: on top of the local bursaries above, students paying £3,225 tuition fees could also receive another university bursary based on your household income. Household income university bursary: £0–£25,000, £800; £25,001–£35,000, £500; £35,001–£50,000, £200.
- For more information: www.derby.ac.uk

## University of Dundee
- Tuition fees for non-Scottish domiciled students for 2009/10: £1,820 pa (£2,895 for Medicine). If you are a Scottish-domiciled first degree student you are eligible for your tuition fees to be covered by the Scottish government. Scottish students should apply to the SAAS to cover this cost. Students from England, Wales and Northern Ireland should apply for a Tuition Fee Loan to Student Finance England, Student Finance Wales, and Student Finance Northern Ireland as appropriate. Students from elsewhere in the EU should contact the SAAS.

• The RUK bursary has been introduced for students normally resident in England, Wales or Northern Ireland only, studying at a Scottish university, who would otherwise have been eligible for a £319 national minimum bursary (i.e. in receipt of full Maintenance Grant) had they studied at a university in the rest of the UK. The RUK bursary is currently worth around £310.

• Fees for placement year and year abroad are normally 50 per cent of full-time fee.

• Chancellor's scholarships worth £1,000 a year to UK students who enter at Level 2. Scholarship holders will normally receive a maximum of £3,000 over 3 years.

• Subject scholarships and bursaries available in many subjects.

• For more information: www.dundee.ac.uk

## Durham University

• In receipt of full Maintenance Grant: £1,300 Durham Grant.

• Tuition fees (2009): £3,225.

• Placement year and year abroad tuition fee will be 50 per cent.

• Durham Grant Scheme (Band 1). Awards will be made to all eligible full-time home undergraduates with a household income of below £18,500 per annum.

• Durham Grant Scheme (Band 1 NE). Awards will be made to all eligible full-time home undergraduate students. A supplement of £1,285 on top of the Band 1 award of £1,285 payable to students with a household income of below £18,500 per annum and residing in the north east (i.e. have a home postcode starting with DH, DL, NE, SR or TS).

• Durham Grant Scheme (Band 2). Awards will be made to all eligible full-time home undergraduate students. To be awarded £525 per year, the student will have a household income of below £18,500 per annum.

• Durham Grant Scheme (Band 2 NE). Awards will be made to all eligible full-time home undergraduate students. To be awarded a supplement of £225 on top of the Band 2 award of £525, making a total award of £750 a year; the student will have a household income of below £18,500 per annum and be from the north east (i.e. have a home postcode starting with DH, DL, NE, SR or TS).

• 25 Vice-Chancellor's scholarships for sport, music and the arts, valued at £3,000 each, will be awarded on entry to full-time home undergraduate students who have demonstrated excellence in the fields of sport, music and the arts.

• For more information: www.dur.ac.uk

## University of East Anglia

• In receipt of full Maintenance Grant: £600.

• In receipt of partial Maintenance Grant: £300.

- Sport scholarship up to £1,000.
- Academic achievement scholarship: £500–£4,000.
- Tuition fees (2009): £3,225.
- Placement year tuition fee and year abroad tuition fee: 50 per cent relevant fee.
- A range of scholarships worth £500–£4,000 exist. Some scholarships are reserved for high achieving candidates from lower income households. All focus on academic merit.
- Access scholarship £500; UEA Science Foundation year scholarship £500; UEA Medical Foundation year scholarship £500; Pathway scholarships £500; Vice-Chancellor Prize scholarships £4,000.
- Course-specific scholarships are available. Sports scholarships and music scholarships are available.
- Separate scholarships available for non-UK EU students for academic excellence: £500.
- For more information: www.uea.ac.uk

## University of East London
- In receipt of full Maintenance Grant: £319.
- Sport scholarship: £1,000.
- Academic achievement scholarship: £1,000.
- Tuition fees (2009): £3,225.
- Placement year tuition fee (2008): £1,570.
- Year abroad tuition fee (2008): £3,145.
- UEL Progress Bursary: £500 for completing first year; £300 for completing second year; £300 for completing third year. Bursary also available to all EU students.
- 200 achievement scholarships a year for academic, sporting and performance arts achievement.
- 50 refugee scholarships to cover the difference between home and overseas fees.
- In kind benefits include books, equipment, fees for field trips (package valued at £750 over three years).
- For more information: www.uel.ac.uk

## Edge Hill University
- In receipt of full Maintenance Grant: £500
- Progression bursary: £500
- Sport scholarship: £2,000
- Academic achievement scholarship: £500
- Tuition fees (2009): £3,225.
- The university ranks top in the North West, and in the top 10 institutions nationally, for re-investing tuition fees on students, with £1.9m spent on scholarships, bursaries and outreach activities in 2007.

- Families earning less than £25,000 pa: £500.
- Four disadvantaged student bursaries from Helena Kennedy Foundation: £1,000.
- Entrance scholarships: £2,000 over three years for undergraduates in the areas of creative arts, online, performing arts, sports, volunteering and preparation for higher education.
- Academic achievement scholarship: £500.
- Jesse Jackson Scholarship (new for 2009/10): £1,000.
- Professor Tanya Byron Scholarship (new for 2009/10): £1,000.
- Fee remission for siblings: £1,000.
- Care leavers are awarded an annual bursary: £750.
- All students liable to pay the variable rate fee (£3,225) receive a £200 a year credit on a UNICARD to be spent at specified retail outlets on course-related materials.
- For more information: www.edgehill.ac.uk

## University of Edinburgh

- Tuition fees for non-Scottish domiciled students for 2009/10: £1,820 pa (£2,895 for Medicine). If you are a Scottish-domiciled first degree student you are eligible for your tuition fees to be covered by the Scottish government. Scottish students should apply to the SAAS to cover this cost. Students from England, Wales and Northern Ireland should apply for a Tuition Fee Loan to Student Finance England, Student Finance Wales, and Student Finance Northern Ireland as appropriate. Students from elsewhere in the EU should contact the SAAS.
- The RUK bursary has been introduced for students normally resident in England, Wales or Northern Ireland only, studying at a Scottish university, who would otherwise have been eligible for a £319 national minimum bursary (i.e. in receipt of full Maintenance Grant) had they studied at a university in the rest of the UK. The RUK bursary is currently worth around £310.
- Fees for placement year and year abroad are normally 50 per cent of full-time fee.
- Over 180 Entrance bursaries of between £1,000–£2,500 pa for students from schools or colleges in the UK whose financial or personal circumstances might prevent them from entering higher education. 90 bursaries of £1,000 are available to first year undergraduate UK students living in university accommodation. The Centre for Sport and Exercise offers a substantial programme of education, support services and funding for outstanding student athletes who are selected onto the Sports Bursary Programme.
- Industrial scholarships within the Schools of Engineering & Electronics, Informatics and Chemistry of £1,000. Opportunities to undertake a paid work placement over the summer months are also available.
- For more information: www.ed.ac.uk

## Edinburgh Napier University

• Tuition fees for non-Scottish domiciled students for 2009/10: £1,820 pa (£2,895 for Medicine). If you are a Scottish-domiciled first degree student you are eligible for your tuition fees to be covered by the Scottish government. Scottish students should apply to the SAAS to cover this cost. Students from England, Wales and Northern Ireland should apply for a Tuition Fee Loan to Student Finance England, Student Finance Wales, and Student Finance Northern Ireland as appropriate. Students from elsewhere in the EU should contact the SAAS.

• The RUK bursary has been introduced for students normally resident in England, Wales or Northern Ireland only, studying at a Scottish university, who would otherwise have been eligible for a £319 national minimum bursary (i.e. in receipt of full Maintenance Grant) had they studied at a university in the rest of the UK. The RUK bursary is currently worth around £310. To be eligible, students must be in either the first or second year of a full-time undergraduate course and must be in receipt of the full Maintenance Grant/Welsh Assembly Learning Grant from their local education authority or education and library board. Students studying on a nursing programme are not eligible to apply.

• Discretionary Fund (previously known as the Hardship Fund): most students from Scotland, England, Wales and Northern Ireland are eligible to apply to the Discretionary Fund in times of financial difficulty. Students studying on a nursing programme are not eligible to apply.

• Childcare Fund: financial help may be available with the cost of formal, registered childcare. Nursing and Midwifery students and all EU and international students – grants to cover up to 50 per cent of childcare costs (max. award is £200 per child per month). Full-time undergraduate and postgraduate students (UK only) – grants to cover up to 80 per cent of childcare costs. All part-time students – help with childcare costs may be available. All childcare awards are calculated after deduction of any financial support received for childcare from any other source.

• A limited number of grants from trust funds and scholarships.

• For more information: www.napier.ac.uk

## University of Essex

• In receipt of full Maintenance Grant: £319.

• In receipt of partial Maintenance Grant: sliding scale so that Maintenance Grant plus bursary equals tuition fee of £3,225.

• Shortage subjects scholarship.

• Sport scholarship.

• Tuition fees (2009): £3,225.

• Foundation year tuition fee: £1,225.
• Placement year and year abroad tuition fee will be 50 per cent of the relevant tuition fee.
• For students in receipt of partial Maintenance Grant the Essex Bursary is intended to bridge the gap between the Maintenance Grant and the tuition fee with a bursary.
• Maths scholarship.
• For more information: www.essex.ac.uk

## University of Exeter

• Bursaries: £1,500 for incomes below £25,000; £750 for incomes between £25,001 and £35,000.
• Sport scholarship: £1,000.
• Shortage subject scholarship: Science subjects up to £3,000.
• Academic achievement scholarship: Vice Chancellor's Excellence Scholarship: £5,000.
• Tuition fees (2009): £3,225.
• Placement year and year abroad tuition fee 50 per cent of the full-time tuition fee.
• 23 per cent of additional fee income earmarked for bursaries.
• Up to 25 Jubilee and Millhayes Science Scholarships worth £2,000-£3,000 pa for students on three and four year science and engineering programmes.
• 10 Vice-Chancellor's Excellence scholarships worth £5,000 a year for exceptional students who, in addition to academic excellence, demonstrate achievement and continued commitment to at least one of the following areas: volunteering, leadership, entrepreneurship, exceptional talent in music, the arts or sport outside their field of study.
• Sports scholarships for students of outstanding sporting ability who show evidence of achievement or potential at national level. Worth up to £1,000 a year for sporting expenses, sports mentoring/training.
• For more information: www.exeter.ac.uk

## University of Glamorgan

• Tuition fees (2009): £3,225.
• Students from Wales will be eligible for a non means-tested Fee Grant (£1,940) from the Welsh Assembly government towards the cost of tuition fees.
• Placement year/year abroad tuition fee will be 50 per cent (except Erasmus).
• Welsh National Bursary of £319 (2008) available to eligible UK students with household incomes below threshold of £18,370.
• Entry scholarship worth £3,000 for eligible students with 300 or

more UCAS tariff points obtained from A levels or equivalent. Terms and conditions apply.
• Residential allowance worth £1,500 for eligible students who normally live more than 45 miles away from the university's main campus at Treforest. Terms and conditions apply.
• Sports scholarship for potential elite athletes who are competing at national and international level in their sport.
• For more information: www.glam.ac.uk

## University of Glasgow
• Tuition fees for non-Scottish domiciled students for 2009/10: £1,820 pa (£2,895 for Medicine). If you are a Scottish-domiciled first degree student you are eligible for your tuition fees to be covered by the Scottish government. Scottish students should apply to the SAAS to cover this cost. Students from England, Wales and Northern Ireland should apply for a Tuition Fee Loan to Student Finance England, Student Finance Wales, and Student Finance Northern Ireland as appropriate. Students from elsewhere in the EU should contact the SAAS.
• The RUK bursary has been introduced for students normally resident in England, Wales or Northern Ireland only, studying at a Scottish university, who would otherwise have been eligible for a £319 national minimum bursary (i.e. in receipt of full Maintenance Grant) had they studied at a university in the rest of the UK. The RUK bursary is currently worth around £310. Students must be in either the first or second year of a full-time undergraduate course and must be in receipt of the full Maintenance Grant/Welsh Assembly Learning Grant from their local education authority or education and library board. Students studying on a nursing programme are not eligible to apply.
• Fees for placement year and year abroad are normally 50 per cent of full-time fee.
• 50 talent scholarships worth £1,000 a year are awarded annually to high achieving new entrants living in the UK who could face financial difficulties.
• For more information: www.gla.ac.uk

## Glasgow Caledonian University
• Tuition fees for non-Scottish domiciled students for 2009/10: £1,820 pa (£2,895 for Medicine). If you are a Scottish-domiciled first degree student you are eligible for your tuition fees to be covered by the Scottish government. Scottish students should apply to the SAAS to cover this cost. Students from England, Wales and Northern Ireland should apply for a Tuition Fee Loan to Student Finance England, Student Finance Wales, and Student Finance Northern Ireland as appropriate. Students from elsewhere in the EU should contact the SAAS.

• The RUK bursary has been introduced for students normally resident in England, Wales or Northern Ireland only, studying at a Scottish university, who would otherwise have been eligible for a £319 national minimum bursary (i.e. in receipt of full Maintenance Grant) had they studied at a university in the rest of the UK. The RUK bursary is currently worth around £310. Students must be in either the first or second year of a full-time undergraduate course and must be in receipt of the full Maintenance Grant/Welsh Assembly Learning Grant from their local education authority or education and library board. Students studying on a nursing programme are not eligible to apply.

• Fees for placement year and year abroad are normally 50 per cent of full-time fee.

• Magnus Magnusson Scholarships: awards of up to £5,000 to students in their second year upwards. Applications from any discipline and from any part of the university or for almost any kind of proposal that will help individuals to reach their dreams are welcome. However, judges will be especially pleased to receive applications from areas relating to any of Magnus Magnusson's personal interests, including the media, history, language, literature and the natural environment. Applicants must demonstrate achievement in their chosen area, and have a clear plan to take their work forward.

• Hardship and Childcare Funds to which UK undergraduate students in need may apply.

• A range of scholarships for undergraduate students in specific subjects, for sports excellence, etc.

• For more information: www.caledonian.ac.uk

## University of Gloucestershire
• In receipt of full Maintenance Grant: £319.
• Living in region bursary.
• Progressing from outreach bursary.
• Sport scholarship.
• Academic achievement scholarship.
• Tuition fees (2009): £3,225.
• Placement year tuition fee will be around £900.
• A one-off payment of £1,025 is available if the student attended a Compact partner school. If the student is in receipt of a full Maintenance Grant they will continue to receive a payment in years two and three.
• Academic scholarship of up to £515 available to those students who gain 360 UCAS points or more.
• Sports scholarship scheme to be announced.
• Music scholarship and bursary to be announced.
• For more information: www.glos.ac.uk

## Glyndwr University

• A bursary of up to £1,000 offered to all full-time undergraduates – based on three different levels according to household income.
• Excellence scholarships of £1,000 available for students presenting 300 points and applying through UCAS by the 15 January deadline.
• Scholarship of £1,000 pa to study full time on a Masters or PhD programme.
• All Welsh domiciled students receive a Welsh Assembly Fee Remission Grant of £1,890.
• Gifted athletes and others may be eligible for a Sports bursary.
• In line with Frank Buttle Trust accreditation, a scholarship is available to qualifying care leavers of £1,000 per year of study.
• For more information: www.glyndwr.ac.uk

## Goldsmiths, University of London

• In receipt of full Maintenance Grant: £1,000 max.
• In receipt of partial Maintenance Grant: up to £500.
• Living in region scholarship.
• Progressing from outreach scholarship.
• Academic achievement scholarship: £500–£5,000.
• Tuition fees (2009): £3,225.
• Part-time tuition fee will be about 50 per cent of the full-time rate.
• Goldsmiths Bursary worth up to £1,000 pa available to all students who start their studies in September 2009 and are receiving the full Higher Education Maintenance Grant and have a household income below £19,000.
• The Student Residential Hardship Bursary Scheme offers students from low-income families financial help with hall of residence accommodation fees.
• Various scholarships for academic excellence, including the Warden's Scholarship worth £5,000 and the excellence scholarships worth £500 pa awarded by each academic department to the best new entrant based on A level or equivalent scores.
• Access to Goldsmiths Scholarship Scheme for up to 32 applicants from local schools and colleges: £500 pa.
• Rostropovich Scholarships worth £500 a year awarded to string players on the BMus in Music.
• For more information: www.goldsmiths.ac.uk

## University of Greenwich

• Academic achievement scholarship: £500.
• Progressing from outreach scholarship.
• Tuition fees (2009): £2,900, except for Pharmacy degree course (£3,225).

• A wide range of bursaries including Access to Higher Education Bursaries, Care leavers' Bursaries, Mature Student Bursaries, Partnership Progression Bursaries, Progression Bursaries, Academic Achievement Bursaries.

• Bursary of £500 a year for home students with UCAS tariff scores in excess of 300 (excluding AS levels), as well as mature full-time student cash bursaries of £500 a year for home students over the age of 25 on 1 September of year of entry, who qualify for means-tested government grants.

• For more information: www.gre.ac.uk

## Harper Adams University College

• In receipt of full Maintenance Grant: £1,000.
• In receipt of partial Maintenance Grant: up to £750.
• Tuition fees (2009): £3,225.
• For more information: www.harper-adams.ac.uk

## Heriot-Watt University

• Tuition fees for non-Scottish domiciled students for 2009/10: £1,820 pa (£2,895 for Medicine). If you are a Scottish-domiciled first degree student you are eligible for your tuition fees to be covered by the Scottish government. Scottish students should apply to the SAAS to cover this cost. Students from England, Wales and Northern Ireland should apply for a Tuition Fee Loan to Student Finance England, Student Finance Wales, and Student Finance Northern Ireland as appropriate. Students from elsewhere in the EU should contact the SAAS.

• The RUK bursary has been introduced for students normally resident in England, Wales or Northern Ireland only, studying at a Scottish university, who would otherwise have been eligible for a £319 national minimum bursary (i.e. in receipt of full Maintenance Grant) had they studied at a university in the rest of the UK. The RUK bursary is currently worth around £310.

• Fees for placement year and year abroad are normally 50 per cent of full-time fee.

• A number of scholarships of £500 pa for four/five years of study are available, with preference given to study of subjects in Science and Engineering.

• Scholarships in Engineering and Physical Sciences of £500 a year for up to 5 years are offered for female students.

• Sports scholarship.

• The Alumni Fund Scholarships at £500 pa for four to five years for UK/EU students.

• Annual music scholarships for instrumentalists and singers applying for a course.

- Sports scholarships
- For more information: www.undergraduate.hw.ac.uk

## University of Hertfordshire
- In receipt of full Maintenance Grant: £1,000.
- Shortage subjects scholarship.
- Academic achievement scholarship.
- Tuition fees (2009): £3,225.
- Fees for placement year and year abroad are normally 50 per cent of full-time fee.
- Two types of Chancellor's scholarship: The Chancellor's Entrepreneurial and Excellence Scholarship, worth £3,000 pa for the duration of a course; and the Chancellor's Gifted and Talented Scholarship, worth £2,000 pa for the duration of a course.
- Science and Engineering scholarships (worth up to £3,000 over 3–4 years) on certain science and engineering degrees available to every student who achieves at least 280 UCAS points and accepts a place from year one on one of the specified degree programmes.
- 135 externally funded scholarships, sponsored by a range of companies including Tesco and T-Mobile as well as individuals.
- For more information: www.herts.ac.uk

## Heythrop College, University of London
- In receipt of full Maintenance Grant: 50 per cent value of the Maintenance Grant.
- In receipt of partial Maintenance Grant: 50 per cent value of the Maintenance Grant.
- All undergraduate students in receipt of Maintenance Grant of up to £2,835 will receive bursary funding of 50 per cent of their Maintenance Grant.
- Tuition fees (2009): £3,225.
- For more information: www.heythrop.ac.uk

## University of Huddersfield
- In receipt of full Maintenance Grant: £500.
- Tuition fees (2009): £3,225.
- No fee to be charged for placement year.
- Bursaries open to all EU students.
- 24 per cent of additional fee income to be earmarked for bursaries.
- For more information: www.hud.ac.uk

## University of Hull
- In receipt of full Maintenance Grant: £1,000.
- In receipt of partial Maintenance Grant: £500–£1,000.

- Living in specified postcodes bursary.
- Academic achievement scholarship: £3,000.
- Tuition fees (2009): £3,225.
- Placement year and year abroad tuition fee: £1,610.
- For more information: www.hull.ac.uk

## Imperial College London
- In receipt of full Maintenance Grant (2009): £3,000.
- In receipt of partial Maintenance Grant on a sliding scale up to £2,000.
- Academic achievement scholarship.
- Sport scholarship.
- Tuition fees (2009): £3,225.
- Placement year and year abroad tuition fee approximately 50 per cent of full-time fee.
- Home students only eligible for awards.
- Additional £300 for students who qualify for the maximum Study Support Bursary and attain three A levels at grade A.
- 29 per cent of additional fee income to be earmarked for bursaries.
- For more information: www3.imperial.ac.uk

## Keele University
- In receipt of full Maintenance Grant: £800.
- Progressing from outreach bursary.
- Academic achievement scholarship.
- Tuition fees (2009): £3,225.
- The university provides a range of bursaries and scholarships, all of which are competitive.
- Keele Bursary of £800 for all UK undergraduate students in receipt of full Maintenance Grant who enrol in September 2009 and pay the full fee of £3,225, except students in receipt of other public funding, e.g. BA Social Work, all Nursing and Midwifery courses, and BSc Physiotherapy.
- Keele Scholarship worth £1,000 for students in receipt of full or partial Maintenance Grant with gross annual household income below £40,000 who obtain three grade As at A level or equivalent tariff points. Students must also make Keele their first or insurance choice.
- KeeleLink Award worth £400 for students enrolling from partner school or college. Conditions apply.
- Care Leavers' Bursary: £1,000 in year one rising to £2,000 in the final year, subject to satisfactory completion of the course. Conditions apply.
- For more information: www.keele.ac.uk

## University of Kent
- In receipt of full Maintenance Grant: £1,000.
- In receipt of partial Maintenance Grant: £250–£1,000.
- Tuition fees (2009): £3,225.
- Placement year and year abroad tuition fees will be approximately £780.
- 20 scholarships for Academic Excellence worth £1,000 a year each.
- 44 Partner Schools and Colleges scholarships worth £1,000 a year each.
- Music scholarships worth £1,000 per year for excellence and commitment to music.
- Sports scholarships worth £250–£5,000 for excellence and commitment to sport.
- Additional sports scholarships of between £2,000–£2,500 pa awarded in partnership with Kent County Cricket Club, Canterbury Rugby Club, Canterbury Men's and Ladies' Hockey Clubs, and Old Bordenian Men's Hockey Club.
- A condition of holding a bursary is attendance at a student support programme, e.g. financial counselling.
- For more information: www.kent.ac.uk

## King's College London
- In receipt of full Maintenance Grant: £1,350.
- In receipt of partial Maintenance Grant: sliding scale up to £1,050.
- Academic achievement scholarship.
- Tuition fees (2009): £3,225.
- King's Scholarships (Myscholarship): 40 to be offered at £1,800 to undergraduate students who excel on their programme of study.
- Eligibility for bursaries to be assessed using LA means-testing process.
- For more information: www.kcl.ac.uk

## Kingston University
- In receipt of full Maintenance Grant: £310–£1,000.
- In receipt of partial Maintenance Grant: £310–£1,000.
- Progressing from outreach bursary.
- Tuition fees (2009): £3,225.
- Placement year fee will be around £610. Fees for year abroad will be around £1,535.
- Every student entering the university as a member of the local Compact Scheme will receive an extra £300 a year.
- 25 per cent of additional fee income to be earmarked for bursaries.
- For more information: www.kingston.ac.uk

## University of Wales, Lampeter
- In receipt of full Maintenance Grant: £305.
- Academic achievement scholarship.

- Tuition fees (2009): £3,225.
- Students living in Wales will be eligible for a Welsh Assembly Fee Remission Grant of £1,940 thus reducing the tuition fee to £1,225.
- Placement year/year abroad tuition fee will be £600.
- For more information: www.lamp.ac.uk

## Lancaster University

- In receipt of full Maintenance Grant: £1,315.
- In receipt of partial Maintenance Grant: £0–£500.
- Academic achievement scholarship.
- Tuition fees (2009): £3,225.
- Placement year tuition fee (2008): £625.
- Year abroad tuition fee (2008) £1570.
- All UK applicants are offered the opportunity of winning a scholarship worth £1,000 if they achieve specified examination grades.
- Scholarships are in addition to any bursaries awarded to students.
- Eligibility for bursaries is on basis of LEA financial assessments.
- For more information: www.lancs.ac.uk

## University of Leeds

- In receipt of full Maintenance Grant: £1,540.
- In receipt of partial Maintenance Grant: sliding scale up to £1,335.
- Living in specified postcodes scholarship.
- Progressing from outreach scholarship.
- Tuition fees (2009): £3,225.
- Foundation year tuition fee: £1,285; placement year and year abroad tuition fees £860.
- Targeted scholarship scheme to attract new UK first generation students from low-income households including those on access programmes such as Access to Leeds – available to students receiving full Maintenance Grant. The scholarship is instead of the bursary. Worth £3,000.
- Targeted scholarship scheme to attract students from income backgrounds of £40,000 pa or less, available to those who also demonstrate academic excellence. This scheme is in addition to the bursary. Worth £1,000 a year.
- Targeted scholarship scheme to attract new UK first generation students from low-income households in the Barnsley, Rotherham and Doncaster areas of South Yorkshire. The scholarship is instead of the bursary. Worth £3,000 a year.
- Targeted subject specific scholarship scheme to attract new UK students from low-income households. This scheme is in addition to the bursary. Worth £1,700 a year.
- Targeted scholarship scheme to attract new UK students from low-income households who play sports at a high level. The scholarship is

instead of the bursary. Worth £1,540, plus free gym membership, coaching and other sports-related benefits.
• A range of School/Faculty specific scholarships: highest value scholarship is worth £6,000 over the duration of a 3/4 year course.
• £8.7 million of additional fee income to be earmarked for bursaries and outreach by 2010/11.
• For more information : www.leeds.ac.uk

## Leeds Metropolitan University
• Tuition fees (2009): £2,000.
• Leeds Met's philosophy of charging less in tuition fees than most universities and so obviating the need for a bursary scheme makes it almost unique.
• Placement year tuition fee will be £500; year abroad tuition fee will be £2,000, i.e. the full time tuition fee.
• Leeds Met Bursary Scheme will continue to offer discretionary Hardship awards of up to £2,000 over 3 years to 22 students each year.
• A range of sporting scholarships.
• For more information: www.lmu.ac.uk

## University of Leicester
• In receipt of full Maintenance Grant: £1,019–1,319.
• In receipt of partial Maintenance Grant: sliding scale up to £400.
• Academic achievement scholarship: £1,000.
• Tuition fees (2009): £3,225.
• Bursaries available to UK students only.
• Subject-specific scholarships of £1,000 for students achieving at least ABB at A level or equivalent.
• Hardship Fund of £100,000 a year.
• For more information: www.le.ac.uk

## University of Lincoln
• In receipt of full Maintenance Grant: £600.
• In receipt of partial Maintenance Grant: up to £370.
• Tuition fees (2009): £3,225.
• Placement year and year abroad tuition fee will be around £650.
• A minimum of £2 million of additional fee income earmarked for bursaries for those in receipt of Maintenance Grant.
• For more information: www.lincoln.ac.uk

## University of Liverpool
• In receipt of full Maintenance Grant: £1,400.
• Living in region bursary.
• Living in specified postcodes bursary.
• Shortage subjects scholarship £1,500.

- Academic achievement bursary.
- Sport scholarship.
- Tuition fees (2009): £3,225.
- Placement year and year abroad tuition fee will be about £625.
- Liverpool Opportunity and Achievement Scholarship worth £4,000, subject to meeting criteria. Students must be home students from household earning less than £20,817 (2007/08 figures) pa, liable to pay tuition fees, and attain AAB at A level or equivalent on entry. The award will be available for subsequent years of the degree programme, subject to satisfactory progress. Students who receive this scholarship will not also be eligible for the Liverpool Bursary or an Attainment scholarship.
- Bursaries will be available to UK/EU students only, subject to means-testing.
- Targeted attainment scholarships in Chemistry, Physics, Engineering, Computer Science, Earth and Ocean Sciences, Biological Sciences, Modern Languages and Geography
- 10 scholarships worth £2,000 a year are available for academic excellence (Alumni Scholarships). The John Lennon Memorial Scholarship and the Hillsborough Trust Memorial Bursaries are awards intended for permanent residents of Merseyside.
- The Sport Liverpool Scholarship Scheme: up to £2,000 pa for student athletes who have already established themselves as a junior or senior international, or are playing at a national or regional level.
- The Liverpool Outstanding Student Award: £10,000 for students graduating in 2009 and achieving a first class honours degree from Liverpool University who have been in receipt of the full Maintenance Grant/Liverpool Bursary or the Liverpool Opportunity and Achievement Scholarship and who are progressing on to either a postgraduate taught or a postgraduate research programme at the University of Liverpool. 10 awards a year will be made.
- The Liverpool Postgraduate Loyalty Award: £1,500 pa for students graduating from the University of Liverpool achieving a first class or 2:1 honours degree and who have additionally been in receipt of the full Maintenance Grant/Liverpool Bursary or the Liverpool Opportunity and Achievement Scholarship and who are progressing on to either a postgraduate taught or a postgraduate research programme at the University of Liverpool.
- For more information: www.liv.ac.uk

## Liverpool Hope University

- In receipt of full Maintenance Grant: £500.
- In receipt of partial Maintenance Grant (household income below £39,333): £500.

- Tuition fees (2009): £3,225.
- Dean's List Scholarships for academic performance and community engagement.
- Hardship Fund.
- Hope Works campus-based employment scheme.
- 29.4 per cent additional fee income will be used for financial support.
- For more information: www.hope.ac.uk

## Liverpool John Moores University

- According to figures published by The Office for Fair Access (OFFA), LJMU spends more than the sector average on supporting lower income and other disadvantaged students.
- If your household income is less than £25,000 you will qualify for a bursary of £1,075* pa. If it is between £25,001 and £50,020 you will qualify for a bursary of £430* pa (*2008 rates). You can spend this bursary as you wish, towards your everyday living costs, to pay off part of your tuition fees or to reduce the amount of Student Loan that you take out. LJMU bursaries are paid automatically to eligible students – you do not need to apply for them.
- If you are a Home student and have studied in higher education prior to September 2009 and are paying the £3,225 fee you will be eligible for a bursary of £1,075 provided your household income is below £18,360. If your household income is between £18,361 and £39,333 you will be eligible for a bursary of £430.
- For more information: www.ljmu.ac.uk

## London Metropolitan

- In receipt of full Maintenance Grant: sliding scale to £1,000.
- In receipt of partial Maintenance Grant: sliding scale up to £775.
- Tuition fees (2009): £3,225.
- Hardship Fund.
- Academic achievement scholarship.
- For information: www.londonmet.ac.uk

## London School of Economics

- In receipt of full Maintenance Grant: up to £2,500.
- In receipt of partial Maintenance Grant: on a sliding scale up to £2,500.
- Tuition fees (2009): £3,225 for home/EU and £12,480 for overseas students.
- The LSE Bursary is awarded to UK students from low-income backgrounds: maximum £2,500 pa. Students in receipt of a partial Maintenance Grant receive a proportion of the £2,500 bursary.
- The Discretionary Bursary worth up to £2,500 is available for UK and EU students who have additional financial difficulties.

- A Job Shop provides part-time employment opportunities for students.
- 25 per cent of additional fee income to be earmarked for bursaries.
- For more information: www.lse.ac.uk

## London South Bank University

- All students (subject to criteria below): £500 in year one; £750 in years two and three.
- Tuition fees (2009): £3,225.
- Placement year tuition fee (2008) £1,570.
- Foundation year tuition fee (2008) £1,255.
- All Home/EU students on full-time undergraduate courses who are liable to pay the full tuition fee are eligible for the LSBU Annual Bursary Scheme which pays £500 in year one; £750 in years two and three.
- £250 graduation bonus for honours graduates.
- 25 per cent of additional fee income to be earmarked for bursaries.
- For more information: www.lsbu.ac.uk

## Loughborough University

- In receipt of full Maintenance Grant (2008): £1,360.
- In receipt of partial Maintenance Grant (2008): £630.
- Shortage subjects scholarship.
- Academic achievement scholarship.
- Tuition fees (2009): £3,225.
- Placement year tuition fee (2008): £625.
- The value of the bursaries is doubled for mature students (21 or over on entry)
- Scholarship scheme for 2009/10: some subject-based merit scholarships offered for applicants meeting specific academic thresholds.
- £3.2 million of additional fee income to be earmarked for bursaries by 2010/11.
- Eligibility conditions apply for bursaries and scholarships.
- For more information: www.lboro.ac.uk

## University of Manchester

- In receipt of full Maintenance Grant: £1,250.
- Living in region scholarship.
- Living in specified postcodes scholarship.
- Shortage subjects scholarship.
- Academic achievement scholarship.
- Tuition fees (2009): £3,225.
- Manchester Guarantee Bursary: £1,250 pa for UK undergraduate students with a household income of £25,000 a year or less.
- Manchester Advantage Scholarship: £3,000 pa for UK undergraduate students with a household income of £25,000 a year or less who attain 3A grades at A level or equivalent.

- Manchester Success Scholarship: £1,250 pa for UK undergraduate students who attain three As at A level or equivalent irrespective of household income. This scholarship is subject specific.
- Access to HE Award: £2,000 pa for UK students from the Greater Manchester area who have progressed to university through an Access to HE programme. An application must be completed.
- Faculties and Schools have also developed a range of scholarship schemes. For further details contact the Admissions Office of the relevant Faculty/School.
- For more information: www.manchester.ac.uk

## Manchester Metropolitan University
- In receipt of full Maintenance Grant: £1,025.
- In receipt of partial Maintenance Grant: £475.
- Tuition fees (2009): £3,225.
- Tuition fees for placement year and year abroad will be approximately £640.
- Additional bursaries of £200 for students returning to MMU to progress to year two of full-time study will be available to those who received the higher bursary in their first year.
- 33 per cent of additional fee income to be earmarked for bursaries and access work.
- For more information: www.mmu.ac.uk

## Middlesex University
- In receipt of full Maintenance Grant: £319.
- Living in region scholarship.
- Sport scholarship.
- Academic achievement scholarship.
- Tuition fees (2009): £3,225.
- Achievement scholarships worth £1,000 to students entering with greater than 360 UCAS points at A2 or equivalent.
- Chancellor's Scholarships for achievement in sporting, cultural or community/cultural areas, worth £500–£1,000.
- Middlesex First Scholarships: 5 x £30,000 to full-time UK undergraduate students.
- Future Gold: Sports scholarships 2 x £30,000 for those showing real Olympic potential for 2012.
- North London First: 5 x £1,000 for each of the four main North London Boroughs – supporting academic achievement, community and cultural contribution.
- Terms and conditions apply to all scholarships.
- 12 per cent of additional fee income to be earmarked for bursaries and access.
- For more information: www.mdx.ac.uk

## Newcastle University
- Bursaries for those in receipt of full Maintenance Grant: £1,280.
- Bursaries for those in receipt of partial Maintenance Grant: £640.
- Tuition fees (2009): £3,225.
- Academic achievement bursary: £500 per year if the student achieves three or more grade A passes at A Level on entry, £200 per year if the student achieves two or more grade A passes at A Level* on entry. (*Or equivalent other qualification.)
- Newcastle University Excellence Scholarships: cash awards, normally available for one year only. Across the university as a whole, we expect to award scholarships for students entering the university in 2009 worth approximately £190,000 in total. There will be 40 scholarships available within Humanities, Arts and Social Sciences, and 110 available within Science, Agriculture and Engineering. There will also be a number of scholarships available within Medical Sciences. The value of the awards varies up to £1,500. The amount and criteria of award will depend on the subject being studied.
- Sports scholarships: up to 20 Recruitment Sports Scholarships and up to 20 Performance Sport Scholarships
- Placement year and year abroad tuition fee is 25 per cent of the full tuition fee, i.e. £806.25.
- Students who are eligible for the Newcastle University Undergraduate Bursary of £1,280 or £640 may also be awarded the Newcastle University Achievement Bursary and/or additional bursaries on taking up their undergraduate student place.
- For more information: www.ncl.ac.uk

## Newman University College
- In receipt of full Maintenance Grant (2008): £800–£1,100.
- In receipt of partial Maintenance Grant (2008): sliding scale up to £500.
- Tuition fees (2009): £3,225.
- For more information: www.newman.ac.uk

## University of Northampton
- Household income up to £25,000: £1,000.
- Household income £25,001–£30,000: £700.
- Household income £30,001–£40,000: £500.
- Tuition fees (2009): £3,225.
- For more information: www.northampton.ac.uk

## Northumbria University
- Tuition fees (2009): £3,225.
- Maintenance bursaries of £319 a year are awarded to those receiving full Maintenance Grant.

- Scholarship awards of between £250 and £1,000 for all first year students, depending on subject studied. The amount received in subsequent years will depend on academic performance.
- More information: www.northumbria.ac.uk

## Norwich University College of the Arts
- In receipt of full Maintenance (2009 entry only): £800.
- In receipt of partial Maintenance Grant (2009 entry only): £300.
- Tuition fees (2009): £3,225.
- For more information: www.nuca.ac.uk

## University of Nottingham
- In receipt of full Maintenance Grant: £1,080.
- In receipt of partial Maintenance Grant: £270–£1,080.
- Students with a household income of less than £44,500 are likely to be eligible for a University of Nottingham Core Bursary of between £270 and £1,080.
- Tuition fees (2009): £3,225.
- Placement year tuition fees and year abroad tuition fees are approximately £1,610. (The fee for a Biosciences Industrial Placement and the Architecture Year in Industry will be considerably less than the above.)
- Additional bursaries are available for students who meet certain criteria, e.g. living in the region, entering through access or vocational qualifications, having dependent children or elderly dependants, lived in care. Some schools, particularly in Science and Engineering, offer subject specific bursaries and scholarships.
- Students in receipt of Core Bursary receive the full bursary for the placement year and the year abroad.
- £2.5 million of additional fee income to be earmarked for bursaries.
- For more information: www.nottingham.ac.uk

## Nottingham Trent University
- In receipt of full Maintenance Grant: £1,075.
- In receipt of partial Maintenance Grant: £360–£665.
- Living in specified postcodes bursary.
- Academic achievement scholarship.
- Tuition fees (2009): £3,225.
- Placement year tuition fee will be approximately £640.
- NTU Nottinghamshire Bursary: up to £265 for eligible students whose permanent home is in Nottinghamshire and have a NG postcode.
- Discretionary Hardship Fund available.
- Scholarship scheme: 50 competitive scholarships of £2,000 a year based on academic performance during the first year of study. Only students receiving the maximum NTU Bursary will be eligible.
- For more information: www.ntu.ac.uk

# The Open University
• For information: www.open.ac.uk

# University of Oxford
• In receipt of full Maintenance Grant: £3,225 (2009).
• In receipt of partial Maintenance Grant: £200–£3,225.
• Tuition fees (2009): £3,225.
• Tuition fee for year abroad is approximately £1,610.
• Different fees rates apply for students studying for a second under-graduate degree.
• Additional one-off award of up to £875 in first year for students from low-income families (household income of less than £18,000).
• Limited number of subject specific bursaries and scholarships available through a competitive application process in first year worth £1,000 per year of course.
• 36 per cent of additional fee income to be earmarked for bursaries by 2009/10.
• For more information: www.ox.ac.uk

# Oxford Brookes University
• In receipt of full Maintenance Grant: £1,560–£1,800.
• In receipt of partial Maintenance Grant: sliding scale to min. £200.
• Progressing from outreach scholarship.
• Academic achievement scholarship.
• Tuition fees (2009): £3,225.
• Placement year tuition fee will be £640. Fees for year abroad will be £1,613.
• Academic excellence scholarships for exceptional achievement (three A grades at A level or equivalent): £2,000 pa.
• Community scholarships for applicants living in Oxfordshire and attending partner schools and colleges: £1,000 pa.
• Hardship Fund available.
• For more information: www.brookes.ac.uk

# University of Plymouth
• In receipt of full Maintenance Grant: £1,015.
• In receipt of partial Maintenance Grant: £300.
• Living in region bursary.
• Academic achievement scholarship.
• Tuition fees (2009): £3,225.
• Fees for placement year £640.
• Care Leavers' Bursary.
• Relocation bursary for mature students.
• Scholarship package includes field trip scholarships of £350 for compulsory field trips; no additional art studio costs for Arts students; Marine sport scholarships worth up to £1,500.

- 25 per cent of additional fee income is set aside for bursaries and scholarships.
- For more information: www.plymouth.ac.uk

## University of Portsmouth

- In receipt of full Maintenance Grant: £900.
- In receipt of partial Maintenance Grant: £600.
- EU students in receipt of full or partial Maintenance Grant: £600.
- Tuition fees (2009) £3,225.
- Placement year and year abroad tuition fee (2008): £625.
- Bursary for 14 local feeder schools and colleges: £300.
- Care-Leavers'-Foyer-Sheltered Accommodation Bursary: £1,500.
- Hardship Fund available.
- 25 per cent of additional fee income to be earmarked for bursaries.
- Award-winning Student Finance team.
- For more information: www.port.ac.uk

## Queen Margaret University

- Tuition fees for non-Scottish domiciled students for 2009/10: £1,820 pa (£2,895 for Medicine). If you are a Scottish-domiciled first degree student you are eligible for your tuition fees to be covered by the Scottish government. Scottish students should apply to the SAAS to cover this cost. Students from England, Wales and Northern Ireland should apply for a Tuition Fee Loan to Student Finance England, Student Finance Wales, and Student Finance Northern Ireland as appropriate. Students from elsewhere in the EU should contact the SAAS.
- The RUK bursary has been introduced for students normally resident in England, Wales or Northern Ireland only, studying at a Scottish university, who would otherwise have been eligible for a £319 national minimum bursary (i.e. in receipt of full Maintenance Grant) had they studied at a university in the rest of the UK. The RUK bursary is currently worth around £310.
- Fees for placement year and year abroad are normally 50 per cent of full-time fee.
- For more information: www.qmu.ac.uk

## Queen Mary, University of London

- In receipt of full Maintenance Grant: £1,078.
- In receipt of partial Maintenance Grant: £861.
- Tuition fees (2009): £3,225.
- Fees for placement year and year abroad: 50 per cent of the regular full-time fee.
- For more information: www.qmul.ac.uk

# Queen's University Belfast
- In receipt of full Maintenance Grant: £1,050.
- In receipt of partial Maintenance Grant: £0–£530.
- Tuition fees (2009): £3,225.
- Tuition fee for placement year is about £640. Fees for year abroad: £3,225.
- Sport and Book Bursary Award (household income up to £33,820).
- 20 per cent of additional fee income earmarked for bursaries.
- For more information: www.qub.ac.uk

# University of Reading
- In receipt of full Maintenance Grant: £1,400 (to be confirmed).
- In receipt of partial Maintenance Grant: £470–£940 (to be confirmed).
- Progressing from outreach bursary.
- Tuition fees (2009): £3,225.
- Placement year and year abroad tuition fee will be about £630.
- Students from Scotland and Wales eligible for bursaries.
- Pre-application, pre-entry bursaries to target groups.
- Outreach schools to nominate candidates for Vice-Chancellor's Bursary scheme worth £2,000 over three years.
- Up to two bursaries may be held by each student.
- Hardship Funds available.
- More than 25 per cent of additional fee income to be earmarked for bursaries.
- For more information: www.rdg.ac.uk

# Robert Gordon University
- Sport scholarship
- Academic Achievement scholarship
- Tuition fees for non-Scottish domiciled students for 2009/10: £1,820 pa (£2,895 for Medicine). If you are a Scottish-domiciled first degree student you are eligible for your tuition fees to be covered by the Scottish government. Scottish students should apply to the SAAS to cover this cost. Students from England, Wales and Northern Ireland should apply for a Tuition Fee Loan to Student Finance England, Student Finance Wales, and Student Finance Northern Ireland as appropriate. Students from elsewhere in the EU should contact the SAAS.
- The RUK bursary has been introduced for students normally resident in England, Wales or Northern Ireland only, studying at a Scottish university, who would otherwise have been eligible for a £319 national minimum bursary (i.e. in receipt of full Maintenance Grant) had they studied at a university in the rest of the UK. The RUK bursary is currently worth around £310.
- Fees for placement year are £910 and year abroad are £1,820.

- Sport scholarships, designed to help students in every aspect of their pursuit of sporting excellence, tailored to individual scholars.
- Academic achievement scholarships, often supported by national and multi-national companies, are offered to students on a range of courses.
- For more information: www.rgu.ac.uk

## Roehampton University
- In receipt of full Maintenance Grant: £500.
- Tuition fees (2009): £3,225.
- £3,000 scholarship if you are a full-time UK or EU student who has achieved 320 points from 3 A Levels or their equivalent within the UCAS tariff at the point of entry. The scholarship is paid over three years.
- Four £3,000 scholarships rewarding students for their commitment to sporting excellence.
- For more information: www.roehampton.ac.uk

## Royal Academy of Music
- In receipt of full Maintenance Grant: £600.
- In receipt of partial Maintenance Grant: up to £400.
- Tuition fees (2009): £3,225.
- Entrance scholarships are awarded following audition on the basis of merit, and other loans and grants are available to UK students attending the BMus Programme.
- For more information: www.ram.ac.uk

## Royal Agricultural College
- In receipt of full Maintenance Grant: £1,615 + £500.
- In receipt of partial Maintenance Grant: up to £1,025.
- Tuition fees (2009): £3,225.
- Over the last five years, the college has invested more than £1.5 million in promising and deserving students.
- Numerous scholarships including RAC Outstanding Achievers' Scholarships and sports scholarships all worth up to £3,000.
- Hardship Fund available.
- For more information: www.rac.ac.uk

## Royal College of Music
- In receipt of full Maintenance Grant: £1,000.
- In receipt of partial Maintenance Grant: up to £1,000.
- Tuition fees (2009): £3,225.
- Entrance scholarships are awarded following audition on the basis of merit, and other loans and grants are available to UK students attending the BMus Programme.

- RCM Euro bursaries of £350 to non-UK EU students assessed to have a household income of under £25,000.
- For more information: www.rcm.ac.uk

## Royal Holloway, University of London
- In receipt of full Maintenance Grant: £750.
- In receipt of partial Maintenance Grant: up to £750.
- Academic achievement scholarship.
- Sport scholarship.
- Tuition fees (2009): £3,225.
- Fees for year abroad £1,535.
- Scholarships of £500 for all in receipt of Maintenance Grant and achieving a certain level in A levels. Competitive Thomas Holloway Founder's Scholarships of £3,500 for 'outstanding' students receiving Maintenance Grant. Competitive Bedford Scholarships of £1,000 for 'outstanding' students.
- 19 per cent of additional fee income to be earmarked for bursaries.
- For more information: www.rhul.ac.uk

## Royal Northern College of Music
- In receipt of full Maintenance Grant (2008): £1,050.
- In receipt of partial Maintenance Grant (2008): £310–£1,050.
- Academic achievement scholarship.
- Tuition fees (2009): £3,225.
- Scholarships are available to students who demonstrate outstanding ability and potential at audition.
- 19 per cent of additional fee income to be earmarked for bursaries.
- For more information: www.rncm.ac.uk

## Royal Scottish Academy of Music and Drama
- Non-Scottish domiciled students fees in year 2009/10: £1,820. If you are a Scottish-domiciled first degree student you are eligible for your tuition fees to be covered by the Scottish government. Scottish students should apply to the SAAS to cover this cost. Students from England, Wales and Northern Ireland should apply for a Tuition Fee Loan to Student Finance England, Student Finance Wales, and Student Finance Northern Ireland as appropriate. Students from elsewhere in the EU should contact the SAAS.
- For more information: www.rsamd.ac.uk

## Royal Veterinary College
- In receipt of full Maintenance Grant: £1,650.
- In receipt of partial Maintenance Grant: up to £1,082.

- Tuition fees (2009): £3,225.
- Merit scholarships of £3,000.
- The college's expenditure on bursaries, additional outreach and enhanced financial advice is expected to be of the order of 34 per cent of additional fee income in 2008/09 and in subsequent years.
- For more information: www.rvc.ac.uk

## University of St Andrews

- Tuition fees for non-Scottish domiciled students for 2009/10: £1,820 pa (£2,895 for Medicine). If you are a Scottish-domiciled first degree student you are eligible for your tuition fees to be covered by the Scottish government. Scottish students should apply to the SAAS to cover this cost. Students from England, Wales and Northern Ireland should apply for a Tuition Fee Loan to Student Finance England, Student Finance Wales, and Student Finance Northern Ireland as appropriate. Students from elsewhere in the EU should contact the SAAS.
- The RUK bursary has been introduced for students normally resident in England, Wales or Northern Ireland only, studying at a Scottish university, who would otherwise have been eligible for a £319 national minimum bursary (i.e. in receipt of full Maintenance Grant) had they studied at a university in the rest of the UK. The RUK bursary is currently worth around £310.
- Fees for placement year and year abroad are normally 50 per cent of full-time fee.
- For more information : www.st-andrews.ac.uk

## St George's, University of London

- In receipt of full Maintenance Grant: £1,295.
- In receipt of partial Maintenance Grant: up to £865.
- Tuition fees (2009): £3,225.
- St George's offers numerous prizes for students undertaking the MBBS degree programme. Most are awarded throughout the course, normally on examination performance. There are also a number of prize examinations held during the year, for which all MBBS students are eligible to enter.
- NHS Bursary for English and Welsh students (NHS funded courses).
- For more information: www.sgul.ac.uk

## St Mary's University College

- In receipt of full Maintenance Grant: £500.
- In receipt of partial Maintenance Grant: £500.
- Tuition fees (2009): £3,225.
- For more information: www.smuc.ac.uk

## University of Salford

• In receipt of full Maintenance Grant: £319.
• Tuition fees (2009): £3,225.
• Statutory bursary £319 pa payable to all students entitled to a full Maintenance Grant.
• Vice-Chancellor's scholarships: £1,000 payable to all who reach the entry standard of grades AAB at A Level; £1000 for all entrants to Modern Languages, Physics and Engineering, who meet the programme and general entry requirements.
• Global Placement Bursary: £1,000 for two semesters spent overseas or £500 for one semester spent overseas.
• Salford Bursary: £500 for all students with a Salford postcode at the time of application who receive a Maintenance Grant (pro rata for partial Maintenance Grant).
• A student may hold only one of these awards at any one time. The highest award for which the individual is eligible would apply. In addition the university offers several special prizes based on a range of criteria. These prizes would not be subject to only holding one award at a time.
• For more information: www.isite.salford.ac.uk

## The School of Pharmacy, University of London

• In receipt of full Maintenance Grant: £500.
• In receipt of partial Maintenance Grant: up to £400.
• Tuition fees (2009): £3,225.
• Supplementary bursaries: up to £500 based on academic performance.
• 25 per cent additional fee income will be used for financial support.
• For more information: www.pharmacy.ac.uk

## University of Sheffield

• In receipt of full Maintenance Grant: £700.
• In receipt of partial Maintenance Grant: £430.
• Progressing from outreach bursary (sliding scale up to £860).
• Sport bursary.
• Priority subjects bursary (up to £1,665).
• Academic achievement bursary (up to £1,665).
• Tuition fees (2009): £3,225.
• Placement year tuition fee for H/EC students (2008): £1,000.
• Year abroad tuition fee (excluding Erasmus): £1,570.
• Additional bursaries for students with a specified household income and outstanding entry grades; amounts vary according to number of A grade A levels achieved and according to subject to be studied: £115–£1,665.

- Additional bursaries for students studying defined priority subjects with a specified household income and with outstanding entry grades; amounts vary according to number of A grade A levels achieved and according to subject to be studied: up to £1,665.
- Bursaries linked to outreach schemes: up to £860.
- 14 per cent of additional fee income to be earmarked for bursaries.
- For more information: www.shef.ac.uk

## Sheffield Hallam University
- In receipt of full Maintenance Grant: £700.
- Progressing from outreach bursary.
- Academic achievement scholarship.
- Tuition fees (2009): £3,225.
- Placement year and year abroad tuition fee will be around £625.
- Sheffield Hallam Partnership Bursary of £300 for students progressing from partner schools and colleges.
- Students who have been in care will automatically have their bursary topped up to £1,500 a year for all years of their course.
- Foyer bursaries of £1,000 available to UK full-time undergraduate students who live in a Foyer or who recently lived in a Foyer.
- Discretionary scholarships: up to £1,000.
- For more information: www.shu.ac.uk

## SOAS
- In receipt of full Maintenance Grant: £860.
- In receipt of partial Maintenance Grant: £420.
- Progressing from outreach bursary: £800.
- Tuition fees (2009): £3,225.
- Year abroad tuition fee will be about £1,610.
- Partner College Bursary: £800.
- 18 per cent of additional fee income to be earmarked for bursaries.
- For more information: www.soas.ac.uk

## University of Southampton
- In receipt of full Maintenance Grant: £1,000.
- In receipt of partial Maintenance Grant: £500.
- Living in region bursary.
- Progressing from outreach bursary.
- Academic achievement scholarship.
- Tuition fees (2009): £3,225.
- Tuition fees for year abroad: £1,500.
- Up to 150 bursaries of £1,000 awarded to students meeting certain criteria who live in Hampshire and Isle of Wight.
- 30 annual widening-participation bursaries of £1,000 to BM6 (Bachelor of Medicine widening access programme) Medical students.

218

Appendix 2

- Many subject-specific scholarships.
- 22 per cent of additional fee income to be earmarked for bursaries.
- For more information: www.soton.ac.uk

## Southampton Solent University

- In receipt of full Maintenance Grant: £1,075.
- In receipt of partial Maintenance Grant: £250–£750.
- Living in region scholarship.
- Progressing from outreach scholarship.
- Tuition fees (2009): £3,225.
- Placement year tuition fee is half the annual tuition fee. Year abroad fee is full annual tuition fee.
- Local scholarships of £250 for students domiciled in Hampshire and the Isle of Wight, and also for students admitted from Compact colleges.
- Various bursaries and scholarships will be available for students who are from local regions, the Channel Islands, overseas and the students on the university's STAND (Solent Talented Athlete Network Development) programme, as well as the university's alumni.
- Various fee discounts may be applied, for example for early payment.
- For more information: www.solent.ac.uk

## Staffordshire University

- In receipt of full Maintenance Grant: £1,000.
- In receipt of partial Maintenance Grant: £500–£1,000.
- Tuition fees (2009): £3,225.
- For more information: www.staffs.ac.uk

## University of Stirling

- Tuition fees for non-Scottish domiciled students for 2009/10: £1,820 pa (£2,895 for Medicine). If you are a Scottish-domiciled first degree student you are eligible for your tuition fees to be covered by the Scottish government. Scottish students should apply to the SAAS to cover this cost. Students from England, Wales and Northern Ireland should apply for a Tuition Fee Loan to Student Finance England, Student Finance Wales, and Student Finance Northern Ireland as appropriate. Students from elsewhere in the EU should contact the SAAS.
- The RUK bursary has been introduced for students normally resident in England, Wales or Northern Ireland only, studying at a Scottish university, who would otherwise have been eligible for a £319 national minimum bursary (i.e. in receipt of full Maintenance Grant) had they studied at a university in the rest of the UK. The RUK bursary is currently worth around £310.

- Scholarships available in six core sports: golf, swimming, disability swimming, tennis, triathlon and football.
- For more information: www.stir.ac.uk

## University of Strathclyde
- Tuition fees for non-Scottish domiciled students for 2009/10: £1,820 pa (£2,895 for Medicine). If you are a Scottish-domiciled first degree student you are eligible for your tuition fees to be covered by the Scottish government. Scottish students should apply to the SAAS to cover this cost. Students from England, Wales and Northern Ireland should apply for a Tuition Fee Loan to Student Finance England, Student Finance Wales, and Student Finance Northern Ireland as appropriate. Students from elsewhere in the EU should contact the SAAS.
- The RUK bursary has been introduced for students normally resident in England, Wales or Northern Ireland only, studying at a Scottish university, who would otherwise have been eligible for a £319 national minimum bursary (i.e. in receipt of full Maintenance Grant) had they studied at a university in the rest of the UK. The RUK bursary is currently worth around £310.
- Fees for placement year and year abroad are normally 50 per cent of full-time fee.
- Bursaries up to £1,000 are available to top sportsmen and women.
- For more information: www.strath.ac.uk

## University of Sunderland
- In receipt of full Maintenance Grant: £525.
- In receipt of partial Maintenance Grant: £525.
- Academic achievement bursary.
- Tuition fees (2009): £3,225.
- Placement year tuition fee will be £250.
- Progression bursaries of £525 for year one to year two, £315 for year two to year three, £125 on graduation.
- Foundation Degree and HND scholarships: Foundation Degree and HND students receive an extra £525 a year on top of the above.
- For more information: www.sunderland.ac.uk

## University of Surrey
- In receipt of full Maintenance Grant: up to £2,050 on a sliding scale.
- In receipt of partial Maintenance Grant: on a sliding scale.
- Living in specified postcodes scholarship.
- Shortage subjects scholarship.
- Academic achievement scholarship.
- Tuition fees (2009): £3,225.

• Placement year and year abroad tuition fee will be about £485 for UK/EU students.
• A range of scholarships worth £1,000 pa are available to students with excellent grades on entry. Specific grade requirements are determined according to the academic discipline. Scholarships are available to students who have not qualified for an entry scholarship but who achieve first class results during their first or second year of study: £1,000 each year.
• Scholarships are available as part of the university's commitment to care leavers and travellers: £1,000 each year.
• 33 per cent of additional fee income to be earmarked for bursaries.
• For more information: www.surrey.ac.uk

## University of Sussex
• In receipt of full Maintenance Grant: £1,000.
• Living in specified postcodes scholarship.
• Ethnic minorities scholarship.
• Tuition fees (2009): £3,225.
• Placement year and year abroad tuition fee is half the annual tuition fee.
• 200 Chancellor's Scholarships aimed at bringing into higher education students from non-traditional backgrounds.
• 20 per cent of additional fee income to be earmarked for bursaries.
• For more information: www.sussex.ac.uk

## Swansea University
• Tution fees (2009): £3,225.
• Students living in Wales will be eligible for a Welsh Assembly Fee Remission Grant of £1,940 thus reducing the tuition fee.
• Fees for placement year and year abroad: £1,570.
• Maintenance Grant: £310.
• 90 excellence bursaries to new UK/EU undergraduate entrants in September 2008, each worth £3,000 over two years. Bursaries available in all subject areas.
• Each year the university offers 10 undergraduate entrance scholarships for students with outstanding sporting talent. Each scholarship is worth £1,000 pa and is renewable for three years.
• A number of the university's departments and schools have also set aside funds or have been given grants to reward academic achievement. These awards range from £400 to £3,000.
• For more information: www.swansea.ac.uk

## University of Teesside
• In receipt of full Maintenance Grant: Teesside Bursary worth more than £3,000 over the three years of study.

- Tuition fees (2009): £3,225.
- Placement year tuition fee: £806. Year abroad fees are variable.
- Care Leavers' Bursary: £1,025 pa for those students who come to university from a care background.
- Excellence scholarships: £1,000 pa for up to three years to be allocated on the basis of academic performance to all students who meet the criteria.
- Subject scholarships:: £1,000 pa for up to three years linked to specific subjects at the university for students who meet the criteria.
- 31 per cent of additional fee income to be earmarked for bursaries.
- For more information: www.tees.ac.uk

## Thames Valley University
- In receipt of full Maintenance Grant: £1,060 (subject to confirmation).
- In receipt of partial Maintenance Grant: discretionary £530 (subject to confirmation).
- Tuition fees (2009): £3,225.
- Placement year tuition fee will be around £1,615.
- For 2009/10 a bursary of £1,060 (subject to confirmation) should be available to home students commencing their studies on full-time undergraduate courses in or after September 2008, who are in receipt of the Maintenance Grant or equivalent and have a household income of less than £25,000. For those with a household income between £25,000–£40,000, a bursary of £530 may be payable.
- For more information: www.tvu.ac.uk

## UHI Millennium Institute
- Tuition fees for non-Scottish domiciled students for 2009/10: £1,820 pa (£2,895 for Medicine). If you are a Scottish-domiciled first degree student you are eligible for your tuition fees to be covered by the Scottish government. Scottish students should apply to the SAAS to cover this cost. Students from England, Wales and Northern Ireland should apply for a Tuition Fee Loan to Student Finance England, Student Finance Wales, and Student Finance Northern Ireland as appropriate. Students from elsewhere in the EU should contact the SAAS.
- The RUK bursary has been introduced for students normally resident in England, Wales or Northern Ireland only, studying at a Scottish university, who would otherwise have been eligible for a £319 national minimum bursary (i.e. in receipt of full Maintenance Grant) had they studied at a university in the rest of the UK. The RUK bursary is currently worth around £310.
- For more information: www.uhi.ac.uk

## University of Ulster

- In receipt of full Maintenance Grant: £1,040.
- In receipt of partial Maintenance Grant: £310–£620.
- Tuition fees (2009): £3,225.
- Tuition fee for placement year £1,570.
- Ulster offers a range of non-repayable Opportunity Scholarships across all subject areas and Faculties.
- For more information: http://prospectus.ulster.ac.uk

## University College Birmingham

- In receipt of full Maintenance Grant: £1,080.
- In receipt of partial Maintenance Grant: up to £648.
- Tuition fees (2009): £3,225.
- No tuition fee for industrial placement.
- UCB offers a range of awards to assist students during their studies designed to complement the bursary scheme.
- For more information: www.ucb.ac.uk

## University College Falmouth

- In receipt of full Maintenance Grant: £850.
- In receipt of partial Maintenance Grant: up to £500.
- Tuition fees (2009): £3,225.
- No tuition fee for industrial placement.
- A range of awards is available to assist students during their studies. Conditions apply.
- For more information: www.falmouth.ac.uk

## University College London

- In receipt of full Maintenance Grant: £1,550–£2,775.
- In receipt of partial Maintenance Grant: 50 per cent of Maintenance Grant value.
- Tuition fees (2009): £3,225.
- Fees for placement year and year abroad are one-third of the undergraduate fee.
- All students in receipt of a Maintenance Grant will receive a UCL Bursary to the value of at least 50 per cent of that grant. (2008 figures: students whose families earn between £14,001 and £16,200 will receive £1,650 a year; students whose families earn between £11,901 and £14,000 will receive £2,200. Students whose families earn less than £11,900 will receive £2,775.)
- Students following a four-year programme, e.g. with a year abroad or the MEng or MSci degrees will, in their fourth year, receive a UCL Bursary equal to 100 per cent of their Maintenance Grant or double the UCL Bursary received in the first three years of study, whichever is greater.
- For more information: www.ucl.ac.uk

## University College Plymouth St Mark & St John (Marjon)

- In receipt of full Maintenance Grant: £319.
- Tuition fees (2009): £3,225.
- A free laptop is offered to all full-time undergraduate students.
- Hardship Fund.
- For more information: www.marjon.ac.uk

## University for the Creative Arts

- In receipt of full Maintenance Grant (2009): £319.
- Tuition fees (2009): £3,225.
- 160 UCreative Scholarships valued at £1,000 pa will be awarded to eligible students to help meet some of the costs of student life. Only students deemed by the interviewing tutor at their interview to have outstanding academic potential will be able to apply. Application forms will be sent following interview to students from households with a family income of under £39,305.
- For more information: www.ucreative.ac.uk

## University of the Arts London

- In receipt of full Maintenance Grant: £319.
- In receipt of partial Maintenance Grant: £1,000 (discretionary).
- Tuition fees (2009): £3,225.
- Fees for placement year (2008): £1,610.
- Access bursary arrangements for 2009/10 are under review. For 2008/9, students receiving a full or partial Maintenance Grant and who are first generation HE students are entitled to apply for a £1,000 Access bursary. Preference will be given to those living in low participation post-code areas.
- For more information: www.arts.ac.uk

## University of Wales Institute Cardiff

- Means-tested bursaries based on household income: £300–£500.
- Entry scholarships of up to £1,000 (Awarding Academic Excellence).
- Sports scholarships.
- Food industry bursary.
- Care Leavers' Bursary.
- Academic achievement scholarship.
- Child care bursary.
- Tuition fees (2009): £3,225.
- Students from Wales will be eligible for a non means-tested Fee Grant (£1,890) from the Welsh Assembly government towards the cost of tuition fees.
- Placement year/year abroad tuition fee will be 50 per cent (except Erasmus).
- For more information: www.uwic.ac.uk

# University of Wales, Newport
- In receipt of full Maintenance Grant: £1,000.
- In receipt of partial Maintenance Grant: sliding scale up to £600.
- Living in region bursary.
- Fees for undergraduate courses (2009): £3,225.
- Students living in Wales will be eligible for a Welsh Assembly Fee Remission Grant of £1,940.
- GAS Bursary to 30 eligible students from GAS partner schools and colleges. Prospective full-time UK students under 25 and dependent on their parents may receive £500 for the first year of their course.
- For more information: www.newport.ac.uk

# University of Warwick
- In receipt of full Maintenance Grant: £1,800.
- In receipt of partial Maintenance Grant: up to £1,800.
- Academic achievement scholarship.
- Tuition fees (2009/10): £3,225.
- Placement year tuition fees and year abroad tuition fees: 50 per cent of full-time fee, excluding Erasmus.
- Warwick Scholarships: £1,800 a year awarded to independent students and students from families with incomes less than £36,001 pa through the Warwick Undergraduate Aid Programme (WUAP).
- A limited number of Alumni and Friends' Named Scholarships: up to £2,000 pa – open to applications from independent students and students from families who receive means-tested benefits or Pension Credit.
- 25 per cent of additional fee income to be earmarked for bursaries.
- For more information: www.warwick.ac.uk

# University of the West of England
- In receipt of full Maintenance Grant: £1,000.
- Tuition fees (2009): £3,225.
- Placement year tuition fees and year abroad tuition fees: around £600.
- Income-assessed bursary of £1,000 available to students liable for the £3,225 tuition fee with a household income of £25,000 or less. Eligibility is assessed by Student Loans Company with the application for student funding.
- Alternatively, Access Bursary of £1,000 is available to students who have completed a recognised (QAA) Access course and are liable for the full tuition fee regardless of their income. Eligibility is assessed by UWE Admissions and International Recruitment.
- Care Leavers' Bursary: £1,000 for UK full-time undergraduate students who have been in care. Eligibility is assessed by UWE Students Advice and Welfare Service.

- Students will not receive a bursary during a placement year or year abroad.
- Around 20 per cent of additional fee income to be earmarked for bursaries for 2009/10.
- For more information: www.uwe.ac.uk

## University of the West of Scotland
- Tuition fees for non-Scottish domiciled students for 2009/10: £1,820 pa (£2,895 for Medicine). If you are a Scottish-domiciled first degree student you are eligible for your tuition fees to be covered by the Scottish government. Scottish students should apply to the SAAS to cover this cost. Students from England, Wales and Northern Ireland should apply for a Tuition Fee Loan to Student Finance England, Student Finance Wales, and Student Finance Northern Ireland as appropriate. Students from elsewhere in the EU should contact the SAAS.
- The RUK bursary has been introduced for students normally resident in England, Wales or Northern Ireland only, studying at a Scottish university, who would otherwise have been eligible for a £319 national minimum bursary (i.e. in receipt of full Maintenance Grant) had they studied at a university in the rest of the UK. The RUK bursary is currently worth around £310. Fees for placement year and year abroad are normally 50 per cent of full-time fee.
- University Hardship Funds available.
- For more information: www.uws.ac.uk

## University of Westminster
- In receipt of full Maintenance Grant: £319.
- In receipt of partial Maintenance Grant: £319.
- Academic achievement scholarship.
- Disabled scholarship.
- Tuition fees (2009): £3,225.
- There will be no tuition fee for any placement year or year abroad.
- Bursaries are open to UK and EU students.
- The university has a large UK and international scholarships scheme.
- 15 per cent of additional fee income to be earmarked for bursaries.
- For more information: www.wmin.ac.uk

## University of Winchester
- Household income under £25,000: £820 bursary..
- Household income between £25,000–£39,333: £410 bursary.
- Tuition fees (2009): £3,225.
- Winchester Scholarship: maintenance award to all full-time undergraduates £175 in year 1, £100 in year 2, £100 in year 3 and £100 in year 4 (if doing a 4-year course).

• Winchester Partnership Colleges Scholarships: £105 for students who come from a University of Winchester Partnership College.
• Winchester Compact Scholarships: £205 for students who are Compact applicants to the University of Winchester.
• Academic achievement award: £4,000. Students studying single honours Archaeology, Archaeological Practice or Theology and Religious Studies with 360+ tariff points from their top 3 A levels (or equivalent qualification) can apply.
• King Alfred Scholarship: £2,050. Available to students from social care institutions.
• For more information: www.winchester.ac.uk

## University of Wolverhampton
• In receipt of full Maintenance Grant: £500.
• In receipt of partial Maintenance Grant: £300.
• Sport scholarship.
• Academic achievement scholarship.
• Tuition fees (2009): £3,225.
• Regional Cashback Bursary: £1,000 (terms and conditions apply).
• Scholarships up to £3,000 for pre-entry academic or sporting achievements.
• For more information: www.wlv.ac.uk

## University of Worcester
• In receipt of full Maintenance Grant: £750.
• In receipt of partial Maintenance Grant: £625.
• Sport scholarship.
• Academic achievement scholarship.
• Tuition fees (2009): £3,225.
• Regional Cashback Bursary: £1,000 (terms and conditions apply).
• Scholarships up to £3,000 for pre-entry academic or sporting achievements.
• For more information: www.worc.ac.uk

## University of York
• In receipt of full Maintenance Grant: £1,400.
• In receipt of partial Maintenance Grant: sliding scale up to £1,400.
• Tuition fees (2009): £3,225.
• Placement year and year abroad tuition fee will be approximately 50 per cent of the standard variable tuition fee.
• Bursaries for the Hull-York Medical School are means-tested but are at a different level (£514–£1,026).
• 19 per cent of additional fee income to be earmarked for bursaries.
• For more information: www.york.ac.uk

## York St John University

- Tuition fees (2009): £3,225.
- York St John Bursary: £540–£1,610 on a sliding scale and means-tested. A household whose annual income is above £25,000 will not be eligible for a York St John Bursary.
- SPARK scholarships are funds raised by former students to support new students. SPARK has provided money for a number of non-repayable SPARK scholarships of £500 a year primarily to alleviate financial hardship.
- Discretionary, non-repayable childcare bursaries may be provided to students who are unable to claim any assistance towards their childcare from the local authority.
- Regional bursaries worth £500 are available to some students who live in the North Yorkshire and Humberside area, are under 21 and from lower income families.
- For more information: www.yorksj.ac.uk

# Useful addresses and websites

## Supporting website

The Complete University Guide
www.thecompleteuniversityguide.co.uk

## General

**UCAS**
Rosehill
New Barn Lane
Cheltenham
Gloucestershire
GL52 3LZ
Tel: 01242 222 444
www.ucas.com

**National Union of Students**
NUS HQ
Centro 3
19 Mandela Street
London NW1 0DU
Tel: 0871 221 8221
www.nus.org.uk

## Applications for student finance

**If you normally live in England:**
*Online applications:*
**Student Finance England**
www.direct.gov.uk/
studentfinance
*Paper applications:*
Download a form from
www.direct.gov.uk/
studentfinance and send to:
**Student Finance England**
PO Box 210
Darlington
DL1 9HJ
Tel: 0845 300 50 90

**If you normally live in Northern Ireland:**
*Online applications:*
**Student Finance Northern Ireland**
www.studentfinanceni.co.uk
Tel: 0845 600 0662

*Paper applications:*
Download a form from
www.studentfinanceni.co.uk and
send to your Education and
Library Board (ELB). To identify
your ELB and find their contact
details, use the ELB finder on the
Student Finance Northern
Ireland website.
More information on student
support policy, admissions to
higher education and general
information:
**Department for Employment
and Learning Northern Ireland
Student Finance Branch**
Room 407
Adelaide House
Belfast
BT2 8FD
Tel: 028 9025 7715
www.delni.gov.uk/studentfinance

**If you normally live in Wales:**
*Online applications:*
**Student Finance Wales**
www.studentfinancewales.co.uk
*Paper applications:*
Download a form from
www.studentfinancewales.co.uk
and send to your local authority.
To identify your LA and their
contact details, refer to the LA
Finder on the website.
**Student Finance Wales**
Princes Park
Princes Drive
Colwyn Bay
LL29 8PL
Tel: 0845 602 8845

**If you normally live in Scotland:**
*Online applications:*
**Student Awards Agency for
Scotland (SAAS)**
www.saas.gov.uk
**The Student Awards Agency for
Scotland (SAAS)**
Gyleview House
3 Redheughs Rigg
Edinburgh
EH12 9HH
Tel: 0845 111 1711

**If you normally live in the EU:**
**a)** To apply for student finance in
England, Northern Ireland or
Wales, download a form from
**Student Finance England**
(**www.direct.gov.uk/
   studentfinance**) and send to:
**Student Finance Services
European Team**
PO Box 89
Darlington
DL1 9AZ
Tel: +44 (0) 141 243 3570
(helpline)
www.direct.gov.uk/studentfinance-
   EU
**b)** For student finance in
Scotland, apply online at
www.saas.gov.uk
Tel: 0141 243 3570

**International students (from
outside the EU):**
**Commonwealth Scholarship
Commission**
36 Gordon Square
London
WC1H 0PF

**UK Council for International
Student Affairs (UKCISA)**
9–17 St Albans Place
London N1 0NX
www.ukcisa.org.uk
Tel: +44 (0) 020 7107 9922

## Student Loans

**Student Loans Company
Limited**
100 Bothwell Street
Glasgow G2 7JD
Tel: 0141 306 2000
www.slc.co.uk

### Applications for Student Loans
See 'Applications for Student
Finance' on page 228.

### Repaying Student Loans
www.studentloanrepayment.
  co.uk
Tel: 0870 240 6298
Tel (from overseas):
+44 141 243 3660

## Bursaries, scholarships and awards

### England:
**Office for Fair Access (OFFA)**
Northavon House
Coldharbour Lane
Bristol BS16 1QD
Tel: 0117 931 7171
www.offa.org.uk

### Northern Ireland:
**Department for Employment
and Learning**
Student Finance Branch
Room 407

Adelaide House
Belfast BT2 8FD
Tel: 028 9025 7715
www.delni.gov.uk

### Wales:
**Higher Education Funding
Council for Wales**
Linden Court, Ilex Close
Llanishen
Cardiff CF14 5DZ
Tel: 029 2076 1861
www.hefcw.ac.uk

### Scotland:
**The Student Awards Agency for
Scotland (SAAS)**
Gyleview House
3 Redheughs Rigg
Edinburgh EH12 9HH
Tel: 0845 111 1711
www.saas.gov.uk

### Charities, trusts and professional institutions:
**Scope**
6 Market Road
London N7 9PW
Tel: 020 7619 7100
www.scope.org.uk

**Skill: National Bureau for
Students with Disabilities**
Unit 3, Floor 3
Radisson Court, 219 Long Lane
London SE1 4PR
Tel and textphone: 020 7450 0620
Helpline: 0800 328 5050
www.skill.org.uk

**Royal National Institute of
Blind People (RNIB)**
105 Judd Street
London WC1H 9NE
Tel: 020 7388 1266
www.rnib.org.uk

The Honourable Society of
Gray's Inn
8 South Square
London WC1R 5ET
Tel:  020 7458 7800
www.graysinn.org.uk

The Royal Medical Benevolent
Fund
24 King's Road
Wimbledon
London SW19 8QN
Tel: 020 8540 9194
www.rmbf.org

The Institution of Engineering
and Technology (IET)
Michael Faraday House
Stevenage
Herts SG1 2AY
Tel: 01438 313 311
www.theiet.org/education

The Institution of Mechanical
Engineers
1 Birdcage Walk
Westminster
London SW1H 9JJ
Tel: 020 7222 7899
www.imeche.org

The Institution of Civil
Engineers
1 Great George Street
Westminster
London SW1P 3AA
Tel: 020 7665 2193
www.ice.org.uk/quest

The Institute of Marine
Engineering, Science and
Technology (IMarEST)
80 Coleman Street
London EC2R 5BJ
Tel: 020 7382 2600
www.imarest.org

The Education Grants Advisory
Service (EGAS)
501–505 Kingsland Road
London E8 4AU
Tel: 020 7254 6251
www.family-action.org.uk

# Part-time and distance learning students

## Funding information:
See 'Applications for student
finance' on page 228.

Open University (OU)
PO Box 197
Milton Keynes
MK7 6BJ
Tel: 08703 334 340
www.open.ac.uk

# Sandwich courses with industrial placements

The Year in Industry (YINI)
Tel: 023 8059 7061
www.yini.org.uk (see website for
regional offices)

# Studying and working abroad

UK National Academic
Recognition and Information
Centre (NARIC)
Oriel House
Oriel Road
Cheltenham
Glos GL50 1XP
Tel: 01242 260010
www.naric.org.uk

**Erasmus Scheme**
British Council
28 Park Place
Cardiff
CF10 3QE
Tel: 029 2039 7405
www.erasmus.ac.uk

**International Association for the Exchange of Students for Technical Experience (IAESTE) UK**
British Council
10 Spring Gardens
London SW1A 2BN
Tel: 020 7389 4114, 4774, 4771
www.iaeste.org.uk

**IAESTE UK**
British Council Northern Ireland
Norwich Union House
7 Fountain Street
Belfast BT1 5EG
Tel: 028 90 248 220 ext. 256, 230

**IAESTE UK**
British Council Scotland
The Tun, 4 Jackson's Entry
Holyrood Road
Edinburgh EH8 8PJ
Tel: 0131 524 5706

**UK Council for International Student Affairs (UKCISA)**
UKCISA
9–17 St Albans Place
London N1 0NX
Tel: 020 7107 9922
www.ukcisa.org.uk

# Health Profession bursaries

**England:**
**NHS Business Services Authority (NHSBSA) Student Bursaries**
Hesketh House
200–220 Broadway
Fleetwood FY7 8SS
Tel: 0845 358 6655
www.nhsbsa.nhs.uk

**Northern Ireland:**
Apply to your local Education and Library Board (ELB)
www.delni.gov.uk/further-and-higher-education/studfin-useful-addresses
(North Eastern ELB for English, Welsh and Scottish students studying in NI, email: studentawards@neelb.org.uk)
Nursing/midwifery: Central Services Agency
Tel: 028 9055 3661

**Wales:**
**The NHS Wales Student Award Unit**
3rd Floor, 14 Cathedral Road
Cardiff CF11 9LJ
Tel: 029 2019 6167
www.nliah.wales.nhs.uk

**Scotland:**
**The Students Awards Agency for Scotland (SAAS)**
Gyle View House
3 Redheughs Rigg
South Gyle
Edinburgh EH12 9HH
Tel: 0131 244 4519
www.saas.gov.uk

# Social Work bursaries

## England:
NHS Business Services Authority (NHSBSA) Social Work Bursary
Sandyford House
Archbold Terrace
Newcastle Upon Tyne
NE2 1DB
Tel: 0845 610 1122
www.nhsbsa.nhs.uk

## Northern Ireland:
Social Services Inspectorate (Northern Ireland)
Student Supporting Scheme
Castle Buildings
Stormont Estate
Belfast BT4 3SQ
Tel: 028 9052 0500
www.dhsspsni.gov.uk
www.niscc.info

## Wales:
Care Council for Wales
Student Funding Team
South Gate House
Wood Street
Cardiff CF10 1EW
Tel: 0845 070 0249
www.ccwales.org.uk

# Career Development Loans (CDL)

## General information:
www.direct.gov.uk/cdl

## Application pack and CDL helpline:
Tel: 0800 585 505 (Learning Skills Council)

## CDL Register of Learning Providers:
Learning and Skills Council in England
Cheylesmore House
Quinton Road
Coventry
CV1 2WT
Tel: 0870 900 6800
www.lsc.gov.uk

## Bank providers:
Barclays Bank Plc
Tel: 0845 607 0080
www.barclays.co.uk

The Co-operative Bank
Tel: 0161 947 7180
www.co-operativebank.co.uk

The Royal Bank of Scotland
Tel: 0800 121 121
www.rbs.co.uk

# Sponsorship

British Armed Forces
www.army.mod.uk

Ministry of Defence
www.mod.uk

The Institution of Engineering and Technology (IET) Power Academy
Michael Faraday House
Stevenage
Herts
SG1 2AY
Tel: 01438 313 311
www.theiet.org/poweracademy

234 Useful addresses and websites

# Gap year

## General information:
www.yearoutgroup.org

## Volunteering/holidays:
**The National Trust**
PO Box 39
Warrington WA5 7WD
Tel: 0844 800 1895
www.nationaltrust.org.uk/
  volunteering

**BTCV Online Shop**
Sedum House
Mallard Way
Doncaster DN4 8DB
Tel: 01302 388 883
www.btcv.org/shop

**Archaeology Abroad**
31–34 Gordon Square
London WC1H 0PY
Tel: 020 8537 0849
www.britarch.ac.uk/archabroad

## Travel:
**STA Travel**
Tel: 0871 230 0040
www.statravel.co.uk

**National Express**
Tel: 020 7529 2000
www.nationalexpress.com

**International Youth Travel Card
(IYTC):**
The International Student Travel
Confederation
www.isic.org

**Youth Hostel Association (YHA)**
Tel: 01629 592700
www.yha.org.uk

**Operation Raleigh**
Tel: 020 7183 1270
www.raleighinternational.org

**Coral Cay Conservation (CCC)**
Tel: 020 7620 1411
www.coralcay.org

## Travel insurance:
**STA Travel**
Tel: 0871 230 0040
www.statravel.co.uk

**Endsleigh**
Tel: 0800 028 3571
www.endsleigh.co.uk

# Working while studying

## Job Shop listings:
**National Association of Student
Employment Services (NASES)**
Tel: 0151 794 4629
www.nases.org.uk

## Student work websites:
www.thecompleteuniversity
  guide.co.uk (see Links)
www.prospects.ac.uk
www.e4s.co.uk
www.work-experience.org
www.justjobs4students.co.uk
www.student-part-time.jobs.com
www.activate.co.uk
www.yougofurther.co.uk
www.summerjobs4u.co.uk
www.bunac.org/uk/workamerica

**Student income tax:**
**HM Revenue & Customs**
**(HMRC)**
Tax office locator at:
www.hmrc.gov.uk

**International students working in the UK:**
**UK Council for International Student Affairs (UKCISA)**
Tel: +44 (0)20 7107 9922
www.ukcisa.org.uk

**National Insurance Office**
Tel: 0845 600 0643 (National Insurance Number allocation)
Tel: 0845 915 4811 or +44 191 203 7010 (General enquiries, non-UK residents)

## Tuition fees

**UCAS – Course search**
Rosehill
New Barn Lane
Cheltenham
Gloucestershire
GL52 3LZ
Tel: 01242 222 444
www.ucas.com

## Accommodation

**Agreements and rights for tenants:**
www.mypropertyguide.co.uk
www.communities.gov.uk
www.adviceguide.org.uk
www.direct.gov.uk/en/Tenancy
  Deposit/index.htm
www.betterrentingscotland.com

www.nidirect.gov.uk/index/
  property-and-housing/buying-
  selling-and-renting-a-home/
  letting-your-property

**Finding accommodation:**
www.thecompleteuniversity
  guide.co.uk ('Students, Where
  to Live'; 'Links')
www.accommodationforstudents.
  com
www.unite-students.com
www.uniaid.org.uk

## Second-hand books

www.amazon.co.uk
www.abebooks.co.uk

## Student insurance

www.endsleigh.co.uk
www.cover4students.com

## Banks

**Comparing student accounts:**
www.moneyfacts.co.uk/money

 **Glossary**

**Access Agreements** Documents submitted by universities to the Office for Fair Access (OFFA) outlining what fees they intend to levy and how much they plan to widen access to university. In Northern Ireland, these documents are submitted to the Department for Employment and Learning; in Wales the nearest equivalent are known as 'Fee Plans', which are submitted to the Higher Education Funding Council for Wales.

**Access Funds** Also known in England as 'Access to Learning Funds', these government Hardship Funds are administered by universities to help students in severe financial difficulty. They are known as 'Support Funds' in Northern Ireland, 'Discretionary Funds' in Scotland and 'Financial Contingency Funds' in Wales.

**Allied Health Professional course** A course leading to professional registration in one of the Allied Health Professions, i.e. Audiology, Chiropody or Podiatry, Dental Hygiene or Dental Therapy, Dietetics, Occupational Therapy, Orthoptics, Physiotherapy, Prosthetics and Orthotics, Radiography, and Speech and Language Therapy.

**Assembly Learning Grant** A Welsh grant to help with living costs, similar to the Maintenance Grant in England.

**Budget** A summary of your intended expenditures and proposed income to cover these expenditures.

**Bursary** A grant of financial or other aid awarded by a university or another organisation. It is normally based on need and/or exceptional ability. Universities often use the terms 'bursary' and 'scholarship' interchangeably.

**Career Development Loan (CDL)** Government funding intended to remove financial barriers to learning and training, available through high street banks. The rate of interest on a CDL is higher than that for a Student Loan.

**Clearing** A system used by applicants to find suitable vacancies on degree courses when they have not managed to secure a university place through their initial application.

**Conditional offer** An offer of a university place which requires that you fulfil certain conditions before you are accepted on the course.

**Deferral** Holding an offer of a university place until the following year.

**Deposit** Money that a tenant is required to pay to a landlord at the beginning of a tenancy, normally the equivalent of a calendar month's rent, as a safeguard against damage. If the property is left in an acceptable state of repair at the end of the tenancy, the deposit should be returned to the tenant.

**Discretionary Funds** *see* Access Funds.

**Distance learning course** A course in which there is separation of place and/or time between the student and the instructor; often based on written correspondence material, audio-visual technology and sometimes summer schools.

**Emergency tax code** A temporary tax code used to calculate the tax you have to pay when you begin earning, before your actual tax code status is confirmed by HM Revenue & Customs (HMRC).

**Erasmus Scheme** An exchange scheme enabling students to study or work for a period of between three months and one academic year in any of the European countries participating in the scheme.

**EU student** A student ordinarily resident in one of the EU countries other than the UK.

**European Credit Transfer and Accumulation System (ECTS)** A standard for comparing the study performance of students across the EU and other collaborating European countries. ECTS credits are awarded for successfully completed studies.

**European Economic Area** A free trade zone covering the countries of the European Union, Iceland, Norway and Liechtenstein.

**Financial Contingency Funds** *see* Access Funds.

**Firm offer** The offer of a university place that you have accepted as your first choice.

**Foundation year course** A first year course designed as a step to a degree course.

**Full-time degree student** Your status when enrolled to study for a degree of a standard duration (three years for most degrees in England, Wales and Northern Ireland; four years in Scotland).

**Gap year** Also known as a 'year out' or 'deferred year', this is usually a year-long break between finishing at school or college and starting university.

**Grant** Financial support which is yours to keep.

**Gross income** Income before deductions are made like tax and National Insurance.

**Halls of residence** The buildings on the university campus or close by where most first year students live.

**Hardship Funds** Public funding administered by universities to assist students in severe financial difficulty.

**HMRC (HM Revenue & Customs)** The government department responsible for collecting taxes, also referred to as the Inland Revenue.

**Home student** A student ordinarily resident in the UK.

**Household income** For the purposes of means-testing, the income of your parents (or that of you and your partner if you are an independent student) after certain allowances have been deducted, such as personal pension payments. Also referred to as 'residual income'. How much you receive in Maintenance Loan, Maintenance Grant and other means-tested support will depend on your household income.

**Income assessment** *see* Means-testing.

**Income tax** A tax on your earned and unearned income over the course of a year, after certain allowable deductions have been made, for example, a Personal Allowance.

**Independent student** Your status if you are aged 25 or over, or are married or in a civil partnership, have no living parents, are permanently estranged from your parents, have supported yourself for three years, or have dependent children of your own.

**International student** Your status if you do not have permanent residence in the UK or the European Union.

**Internship** *see* Placement.

**Loan** Financial support which usually has to be re-paid.

**Maintenance Grant** A grant towards your day-to-day living costs while at university. Sometimes known as a 'Student Grant' or a 'Special Support Grant'. Unlike a Student Loan it does not need to be repaid.

**Maintenance Loan** *see* Student Loan.

**Mature student** Your status if you are aged over 21 at the start of your course (20 or over in Scotland).

**Means-testing** The process of investigating your household income to determine eligibility for financial assistance. Also known as 'income assessment'.

**Minimum wage** The lowest wage that employers may legally pay to employees – usually expressed as pay per hour.

**National Insurance Contributions** Payments made by people in work in the UK towards their future right to claim social security benefits (for example, a state pension and unemployment benefit).

**National Insurance Number (NINo)** A unique number allocated to each UK resident at the age of 16 and used to keep track of your national insurance contributions when you start work and any benefits you receive. You need to have a NINo to apply for a Student Loan.

**NHS Bursary** A grant of financial aid for health professional students, normally means-tested.

**Open University** A university based in the UK which is open to students without formal academic qualifications and which offers distance learning courses.

**Ordinarily resident** You are 'ordinarily resident' somewhere if it is where you normally live from choice and for a settled purpose, apart from temporary or occasional absences.

**Parental contribution** The amount of financial support your parents are assessed to contribute towards your university education based on their household income. Their contribution is treated as part of your student support package.

**Part-time degree student** Your status when enrolled to study for a degree course that extends over a longer period than the standard three years (four years in Scotland) and allows time for external commitments.

**PAYE (Pay As You Earn)** The system whereby income tax is deducted from an employee's salary by their employer and forwarded to the HMRC.

**Personal Allowance** The first portion of income that is tax free for UK residents.

**Placement** Part of a degree course involving work experience or training at an organisation external to the university. Sandwich courses often incorporate a full-year paid placement in industry. Vacation work is sometimes known as a 'placement' or 'internship'.

**Practice Placement Expenses** An allowance payable towards travel and accommodation costs for students on a clinical placement.

**Private university** A university run independently of direct government support.

**Publicly funded university** A university funded in part by the government.

**Residual income** *see* Household income.

**Retail Prices Index (RPI)** An indicator of inflation in the UK measuring the average change, month by month, in the prices of goods and services purchased in the UK.

**Sandwich degree** A degree course consisting of alternate periods of study and industrial placements.

**Scholarship** *see* Bursary.

**Shortage subjects** Priority subjects for attracting students because of a shortage of enrolments on such courses and/or a shortage of people in related careers. Shortage subject courses often attract enhanced financial support.

**Special Support Grant** *see* Maintenance Grant.

**Sponsorship** Financial and other support for an individual student provided by a company or institution, usually involving work experience with the sponsor during vacations.

**Student finance provider** The organisation which deals with applications for financial support in the UK country where the student is ordinarily resident.

**Student Grant** *see* Maintenance Grant.

**Student Loan** A loan provided by the government and administered by the Student Loans Company to cover your university tuition fee (Tuition Fee Loan) and/or your day-to-day living costs while at university (Maintenance Loan). Student Loans are at a very low rate of interest (just covering inflation) and do not have to be paid back until after graduation, once you start earning £15,000 or more.

**Student Loans Company** *see* Student Loan.

**Students' Outside Scotland Bursary** A Scottish bursary similar to the Maintenance Grant in England and available to Scottish students studying at UK institutions outside Scotland.

**Supplementary Grants** Financial aid you do not have to pay back which is additional to the main student funding, for example, the Disabled Student's Allowance.

**Support Funds** *see* Access Funds.

**Tax code**  A code allocated to every person who is paid under the PAYE (Pay as You Earn) scheme in the UK. The code indicates to your employer how much tax to deduct from your salary or wage.

**Tenancy agreement**  A written agreement setting out the terms of a tenancy and the rights and obligations of the landlord and the tenant.

**Tenant**  You are a tenant if you pay a rent in return for use of accommodation owned by a landlord.

**Top-up fee**  *see* Tuition Fee.

**Tuition Fee**  The fee levied by your university towards the cost of your tuition, sometimes known as a 'top-up fee' or 'variable fee'.

**Tuition Fee Grant**  A grant received by Welsh students who choose to study in Wales, which effectively reduces the tuition fees paid by Welsh students.

**Tuition Fee Loan**  *see* Student Loan.

**UCAS**  The organisation responsible for managing undergraduate applications to UK universities and colleges.

**Unconditional offer**  An offer of a place at university that is not dependent on your satisfying further criteria.

**Undergraduate**  Your student status if you have not yet received a first degree.

**Undergraduate course**  A course leading to a Bachelor degree; usually the first level of university study.

**Variable fee**  *see* Tuition Fee.

**Young Students' Bursary**  A Scottish grant to help with the living costs of Scottish students studying in Scotland, similar to the Maintenance Grant in England.

# Index

To buy further copies of
**The Complete University Guide: Student Finance**
at the special price of £5.59,
saving 30% off the standard price of £7.99,
order through our website:
**www.constablerobinson.com/studentfinance**


Also available at *www.constablerobinson.com*
and at good bookshops:
**How to Boil an Egg**
**184 Simple Recipes for One**
by Jan Arkless
price £5.99
*The essential step-by-step guide for those new to cooking*

Jan Arkless's bestselling recipe book has given confidence
to a whole generation of new cooks. All the recipes you need
are here, starting right at the beginning with how to boil an
egg – and then how to poach, scramble and fry it as well.
A new, fully revised and updated edition will be available in
summer 2009, including such new recipes as Hoisin Chicken
Stir Fry, Tabbouleh and Winter Pork Casserole.